To Tamara,
May God bless you + keep you!
Love you much

12/1/18

BUT...HE BRINGS YOU MANGOS

BUT...HE BRINGS YOU MANGOS

MARITAL INSIGHTS FROM SEVEN WOMEN WITH THE COURAGE TO SHARE

The Animus Group

ISBN: 0997066504
ISBN 13: 9780997066500
Library of Congress Control Number: 2016900977
The Animus Group, Accokeek, MD

Acknowledgments

Thank you to the following individuals without whose contributions and support this book would not have been written.

Our husbands for their support and patience; authors Ann Clay and Eric Franklin, whose guidance was invaluable in shaping our writing process and project planning; Greg Moultrie for his honest feedback and encouragement; and our families and friends.

Lastly, we acknowledge each author contributing to this work. Thanks for your honesty, your openness, and your dedication to realizing this book.

PREFACE

BUT... HE BRINGS You Mangos represents the importance of appreciating how your spouse shows you love. We all have our ideas and images about the "right way to show love" and, while our individual needs and how we want to be loved are valid, *But... He Brings You Mangos* is about also recognizing and embracing the many ways that love can be expressed. Your spouse's *Mangos* may or may not be diamonds or roses, a romantic dinner, or expensive gifts; they may well be expressed by taking one's shoes off at the door, washing your car, or making you breakfast. *But... He Brings You Mangos* is about being open to how your spouse shows you love.

Here are instructions for the reader of this book: brew yourself a cup of coffee, pour yourself a cup of cinnamon tea, or get a cup of lemonade or the beverage of your choosing. Find a nice quiet spot for your reading pleasure, and prepare to be encouraged and enlightened. What you are about to read are seven short stories compiled by seven different women as we share our journeys through marriage—in other words, the survival of the "I do."

The authors of these stories are diverse in background, culture, and life experiences. Although varying in race, cultures, professions, age, and years in marriage (from six to thirty-five years), we found ourselves coming together to share a mutual desire and interest in having happy, loving, and lasting marriages. In the hope of helping others to make it through the trials that come with marriage, we embarked on this project; we all had a story to tell.

We choose to value and uphold the sanctity of marriage. Modern culture has skewed the purpose and expectations of marriage so much that when the realities of marriage begin to take shape, many people choose divorce. So you may ask, what is the reality of marriage? The stories in this book depict the challenges, the sacrifices, and the joys that make up a marriage. Most importantly, marriage is an intimate, up-close, sometimes-uncomfortable look at human development, spiritual growth, and our own ability to love, respect, value, and support other human beings (our spouses), even when they are less than perfect. Our journeys are not ones of perfection or rose-colored glasses. They are ones of love, compassion, faith, and commitment. The gift of a lasting marriage is still real, desirable, and attainable despite what today's society and statistics would have you to believe. To those who are married or seeking marriage, we hope that these life experiences encourage you and equip you with the strength and the power needed to unconditionally love another imperfect human being.

Oddly enough, in writing our stories, we learned to appreciate that being connected with another person until death do you part can transform you, heal you, and grow you up. It's not about our husbands; it's about "we the women" and our journey to navigate the challenges of pride, trust, patience, forgiveness, envy, faith, and love through commitment and perseverance.

Thank you for choosing to read this book. We hope you enjoy your coffee and this book, of course, but more importantly, we hope you find a way to enjoy your marriage! It can be done!

Love is Patient, love is Kind. It does not Envy, it does not boast, it is not Proud. It does not dishonor others, it is not self-seeking, it is not easily angered, it keeps no record of wrongs. Love does not delight in evil but rejoices with the Truth. It always protects, always Trusts, always Hopes, always Perseveres.

—1 Corinthians 13:4–7

CONTENTS

Acknowledgments · v
Preface · vii

Chapter 1   By the Power Vested in Me · 1
            Ann Frank (also known as *Michelle Jones*)
Chapter 2   Lord, Is This My Issue or Our Issue? · · · · · · · · · · · · 22
            Charlotte E. Harris
Chapter 3   Will You Love Him? · 37
            Ellen Flowers-Fields
Chapter 4   He's Everything I Asked For and More · · · · · · · · · · · 55
            Gwen E. Schiada
Chapter 5   Through It All · 72
            Royce Slade-Morton
Chapter 6   Journeying toward Your Purpose, Not Jockeying
            for Position   · 80
            DC
Chapter 7   Walking into My Destiny alongside a
            Covenant-Keeping God · · · · · · · · · · · · · · · · · · · 94
            Nonyem Oguejiofor

CHAPTER 1

BY THE POWER VESTED IN ME

At the end of each ceremony, an authority sanctioned to unite two people legally in marriage will say, "By the power vested in me, I pronounce you man and wife." Note that he or she does not say, "By the power vested in me, I will guarantee you will stay married!" Each of us has the vested power to make or break a marriage. The inner Godly strength to follow the path of love and restraint is enormously powerful.

THEME: LOVE AND PERSEVERANCE

GETTING MARRIED? ALREADY married? Know anyone who is married?

Have you ever taken that walk down the aisle or stood before a wedding officiant with flutters in your stomach, pounding in your heart, and precious hopes for dreamy love? You imagine blissful companionship and are excited about creating a future together and being forever joined. Oh, yes, let's not forget lifelong good sex! If you have had such an experience, anticipate one for yourself, or are hopeful for those whose marriage ceremonies you've witnessed, then the next few thoughts concerning marriage are for you! These thoughts and principles are to live by or to share with others.

Many times at the end of each ceremony, a sanctioned authority will unite two people legally in marriage; he or she will say, "By the power vested in me, I pronounce you husband and wife," or some variation thereof. Note that he or she does not say, "By the power vested in me, I will guarantee you will stay married forever and ever!" Happiness thereafter is solely up to you.

Unfortunately, we've heard stories of couples who've had sweet wedding ceremonies, not to mention fabulous reception parties with great food, endless drinks, and more than enough party line dancing for one person to stand. After all of this celebrating, the happy couple divorces or annuls the marriage six to twelve months later. It's no doubt that the couple was in love and happy prior to, or definitely for, that day at least. All too often, the couple was happy but did not know how to keep the euphoria euphoric!

It is not easy to keep the happiness alive while you are connected to a person whom you love but who may be your opposite in many ways. Even if your spouse is not the opposite of you, most likely you both still have different thoughts and ways—unless you are marrying your clone. That's an interesting thought: Could you be married to you? Keeping marital happiness requires a special kind of power and strength. Many people believe achieving and maintaining this type of happiness comes from within. Internal power and strength is a well-accepted notion. People talk about "looking within" all the time. This power is often referred to in many circles as spiritual, kinetic, physiological, philosophical, and even artistic power. Many philosophers, poets, and persons of great achievement and success, as well as *absolutely* men and women of faith, believe in the ability to draw from a personal inner strength or power. Consider these quotes:

1. "Look well into thyself; there is a source of strength, which will always spring up if thou wilt always look."

    —Marcus Aurelius

2. "Strength does not come from physical capacity. It comes from an indomitable will."

    —Mahatma Gandhi

3. "What lies behind us and what lies before us are tiny matters compared to what lies within us."

    —Oliver Wendell Holmes

4. "Your great power lies not on the surface but deep within your being."

    —Roger McDonalds

5. "You have power over your mind—not outside events. Realize this, and you will find strength."

    —Marcus Aurelius

6. "Nothing can dim the light which shines from within."

    —Maya Angelou

7. "We may get knocked down on the outside, but the key to living in victory is to learn how to get up on the inside."

    —Joel Osteen

8. "What we achieve inwardly will change outer reality."

—Plutarch

9. "Become aware of and recognize fully the fact that the Principle of Power within you is God Himself. You must consciously identify yourself with the Highest."

—Wallace D. Wattles

I believe each of us has a power vested within us to aid in making our marriages great. As I mentioned earlier, many people believe in inner strength. They may attribute it to science and adrenaline, the divine universe, or even mind over matter. I believe the power is attributed to all those things. However, I would be remiss if I didn't mention I believe that all those things come from God Almighty. My belief is that this strength is an inner Godly strength designed to allow one to follow a path of love, restraint, and good will.

We also have the power to break a marriage. It definitely takes two to make a marriage great. On the other hand, *one* person alone can make a marriage miserable. Make sure that *one* is not you. I don't believe that the destructive power for evil is from God, even though He may allow it. A person's free will to indulge in destructive behaviors for evil and in disruptive lifestyles is something God disapproves of but will still allow. God's hope is for people to love and trust Him enough to indulge His will. I believe that's why He gives us this inner strength: to do His will. He doesn't force us; however, He will give us the tools to enable us. This inner ability manifested outward is enormously powerful.

Let's stop right here for a moment. Believe it or not, what I am about to share with you was a true aha moment for me that was transformative for my marriage! Let me give you a little background context.

My friends and I were two years into our writing project. We were a very busy group of ladies wanting to share with others our experiences in our marital journeys and hoping to give married women some perspectives that may help them in their marriages. OK. Let's pause a minute. I want to make a point, When we started two years ago, I was going to write about my experience being married to a passive-aggressive husband; the name of that chapter would have been "I Know I Ain't Crazy!" You know, passive-aggressive people tend to tell you one thing and do something totally different, and they leave you to think you're crazy. I now know writing one chapter would not have been enough.

I had a strong inner guide urging me to write something different at this time. It was God! He gave me a new title, "By the Power Vested in Me," with a focus on inner power to guide you, help you, and give you strength to ignore the wrong things and do the right things concerning problems in your marriage. I knew this inner power was real. From time to time, I had used it without much thought. So I began to think about this inner strength and vested power more and more. I did some research, and I began to write down what it is, how it is perceived, where it comes from, and what it could do for you. Yes, all the things you've already read thus far in this chapter. Then I stopped. I could write no more! I tried month after month. At this point, I had nothing! Sometimes, I really felt bad; my friends were writing pages and pages, and I had nothing but a few words.

Meanwhile, my twenty-year marriage was a mess, more than ever before. Up until then, my husband and I were doing relatively well in the getting-along department. I mean my husband and I had already overcome some pretty steep obstacles and still liked each other—OK, we loved each other. But seriously, in the beginning while I was writing this chapter in the book, I was living a pure hell with my husband. Every month, we were having major blowouts over really dumb stuff, stuff so dumb that I no longer remember most of them. Whatever they were, they invoked so much vile emotion on some occasions that we couldn't stand to be in the same room.

Over the twenty years, we'd been through heartache, addiction, a child born with a birth anomaly, financial crises, family issues, and so much more. We had endured all of this, and then we would lose our minds over fights like the one about using my new bedspread comforter set that I purchased in October in preparation for Christmas. I was saving it for Christmas night. It was my gift to myself, and my husband let my daughter and her friends sleep on it, because it was easier than putting my daughter's dirty comforter in the wash! Didn't he get it? I was saving it for Christmas. He let other people sleep on it (like a sleeping bag), and they didn't even appreciate how pretty it was.

Really, he was inconsiderate, but I was a wound-up mess! I'm serious; I felt like calling a lawyer and going to the judge on that one! I was ridiculous. My response to this dysfunction was out of control. There was all this pointless arguing while I was on the book project where I'm supposed to be writing about how to stay married—heck, I wasn't sure if I was going to! One thing after another, we were really going through it. I was complaining like crazy and always mad at him for something.

Oh, I'm sure a little angst was warranted, but I was overboard and out of control in the way that I was dealing with it. I did think I might have to drop out of the book project. I used to have such a good handle on how I handled conflict. I'm a trained mediator, for God's sake. What was my problem? Why was I having all of these breakup feelings now? Aha! I got it! I was a hypocrite and didn't realize it. It sounds bad, but it really was innocent! God had given me insight about vested power; I had begun to talk about it and write about it, but I wasn't doing it!

God needed me to see how this thing could truly work. I researched it and talked about it, but I wasn't living it! I got it. I had nothing to write; while our premise in writing this book was to share our experiences, I had no substantive experience to write about. Once I began to seriously practice what I was preaching, I had plenty to write about. I used the vested power so much that I didn't even have to dig down to find inner strength. It just showed up! Hallelujah! Amen! There was a true transformation in my marriage once I really began to use the power from within.

Shall we continue?

Regardless of one's belief of the origin of the good and productive power of strength within us, the majority of people do believe it exists. The perplexing thought is how many people never think to develop or utilize such power. You might think that if you have access to power, why not use it? As much as I hate to admit it, this was me! I knew all about the *power* of inner strength, but I wasn't using it consistently—or at all in some cases! Consider this: If the air conditioning works and you have paid the bill, why should you sit in a scorching-hot house when you can use the power of electricity to cool the house? Duh. I use this analogy to say that power has been vested to us. The bill has already been paid; why not use it? Turn your power on. Use this power for the good in your marriage. Don't waste time—like I did—being hot, mad, and angry when you can be "chilling out." I could have chilled out during all those unnecessary arguments with my husband. I can't stress it enough: once I stopped talking about it and began *being* about it, I began to write again. So here you go. By using the power vested in you, you can do many things to create euphoria in your marriage.

> **By the power vested in you, you can...**foster peace and compromise in your marriage.
> **By the power vested in you, you can...**submit to giving up control.
> **By the power vested in you, you can...**hold your tongue when you want to lash out at your spouse.
> **By the power vested in you, you can...**have patience when they don't take action as quickly as you would like.
> **By the power vested in you, you can...**love unconditionally.
> **By the power vested in you, you can...**support them even when they do dumb things.
> **By the power vested in you, you can...**have enjoyable sex with your spouse even when you do not feel like it.

Let's explore this idea of vested power and the importance of this wedding-officiant analogy a little more. What is the meaning of "by the power vested"? For the performance of a marriage ceremony, it means that the state has given authority to applicants who want this type of power. In other words, a large entity (the state) gives power to a single vessel to deem marriage legal. In the same regard, a larger source gives individuals power to make marriage meaningful, eternal, fruitful, loving, and happy. Considering this, you might say one exercises vested power at the start even before the actual marriage begins. Choosing the person who will perform the marriage ceremony is a decision that couples face when preparing for their wonderful day. Deciding who has the privilege to speak the first words of encouragement over your life as you are joined to another is powerful. By selecting who will officiate your wedding ceremony, you have already put into action one of the most important things to consider in marriage: the power of spoken words or the spoken word! The Bible states there is life and death in the power of the tongue (Prov. 18:21).

The first person to officially speak over your marriage is of your choosing. Think about it: when we experience difficulties in our marriages, we typically would not want to seek counsel from unwise or ill-informed people but from those who have wisdom and have shown success in relationship building. The same should be true about the person whom you choose to present you with your "until-death-do-you-part" marriage commitment and spoken vows. By the power vested in you, you have authority to make the decision about who speaks significance to you. Who speaks knowledge and value into your marriage? The selection of the vested power of a state-authorized officiant and your inner power begins with you. The officiant may be licensed by the state; however, you have been licensed to love by God if you begin your marriage using vested power. Think about exercising that strength for the good of your marriage.

Now, by the power vested in me, I deem you aware of your vested power, which is not to be abused but is to be used for the preservation of your marriage! You are now licensed to love using your inner power.

Life Gets in the Way: Stuff Happens

Life gets in the way of living happily ever after. Life gets in the way of the flurries of love and romance. At the height of marital bliss, couples get along so well. They are so accommodating to one another. Compromise comes easily, as does overlooking our spouses' flaws. Oh my goodness, there are times when you just can't keep your hands off another due to the explosion of pheromones you've generated (that's scientific). But after a period of time, life's circumstances, decisions, and situations get in the way. In the way of what? In the way of daily marital bliss.

Problems involving sex, the home, food, children, work, money, and communication are often the very things in a marriage that cause the most pain and unhappiness. Many times, this happens because these problem areas are overlooked and or outright ignored.

Sex might become an effort. Routine household decisions—such as what wall color to choose, how often the grass is cut, or even who cuts the grass—might become an effort. Differences concerning the children, avoidance of routine communication, work commitments, and the big one—money issues—might become overwhelming to the relationship. I am not stating these things as a counselor or mental-health or medical practitioner. I am contributing this writing and these examples as one who has witnessed firsthand the aforementioned. I'm more than a witness; I'm currently experiencing these things and have experienced them in the past. My husband and I have endured all of the above and much more. Yet I am still in it for the long haul.

If I were reading this chapter in this book as opposed to writing it, I would naturally ask why in the world anyone would want to stay in such a relationship. Well, I love him. I don't love all his ways, but I love him! I am in it for the long haul because I realize I'm not the only one. I have company. There is a saying that there is nothing new under the sun (that's actually in the Bible: Eccles. 1:9). Everything is in the Bible. The belief that nothing is new under the sun is relevant to this text because it means someone else has been through these trials. I'm sure these issues have some resolution by now. I am not alone in this. Other couples have experienced and will experience such things. I don't express this with glee. Rather, through this discovery, I realized that my husband is the "familiar husband" or "familiar man." There are scores of men who think and act like my husband.

Consider the following examples:

First, my husband wants desperately to do everything himself. He thinks he can. It's not that he can't for some things, but sometimes he won't; he has other priorities, like the "game is on"! Sadly, football, baseball, and boxing have priority service at times in our household. I often suggest that we pay someone to do these things he puts off doing and get it over with. It would be no problem. But "no problem" sometimes becomes a big problem! "No problem" becomes an argument about getting things done efficiently without procrastinating. Does this sound like any men you know?

Second is sex. Men are visual; women are emotional. I do *not* want to be grabbed, poked, groped, or pinched the way a drunken sailor might offer. Need I say more, ladies? How about a little tenderness!

Third, I know I am not the only woman who hides new shoes in the trunks of her car. I know I am not alone.

Men and women are different; however, a number of their problems is the same. Yes, that's why those books such as *Men are from Mars, Women are from Venus*, by John Gray, or *Men are Like Waffles—Women Are Like Spaghetti*, by Bill and Pam Farrel, are so popular. It is because there is much truth to the fact that men have certain ways about them, as do women. Men and women are differently made, and we think differently; therefore, women exhibit similar tendencies just as men demonstrate shared gender-based behaviors. One of my dear friends, Charlotte, often refers to men's shared behaviors as something they learned in "male school" where they majored in "manology."

So it is reasonable to conclude that other women experience some of the same madness in their marriages as I do in mine, primarily due to the "familiar husbands" and "familiar wives" theory. Therefore, I can deduce that some marital problems are familiar as well. OK, I am not alone with these issues. These issues may be considered natural occurrences of marriage. I hate to give up my marriage for something that others have conquered. I know there has got to be a book on these common issues out there somewhere. The Bible states there is no temptation uncommon to man: "No temptation has overtaken you except such as is common to man; but God *is* faithful, who will not allow you to be tempted beyond what you are able, but with the temptation will also make the way of escape, that you may be able to bear *it*" (1 Cor. 10:13).

I interpret this scripture to mean that others are currently going through, or have been through, these same problems. I am not on this island by myself. The question is how you conquer this problem of "life" getting in the way of your happiness ever after. One of the answers would be that we must consider and focus on allowing unconditional love to *stand* in the way of life's path. Use your inner strength to open the door of understanding that life happens. And when "life" happens, love must prevail. Love conquers all.

Difficult Women in Marriage: Do You Recognize Any of These Ladies? What Type of "Wifey" Are You?

I'm sure we've all seen the "unlikely" couple. These are couples who seemingly look unmatched. Note I stated "seemingly." Oh, come on, sometimes we look at the couple in which there is a really tall husband and really short wife and think, "Wow, how do they even..." I am not even going there; you get the picture. Better yet, what of the reverse: a couple in which the wife is remarkably taller than her husband? Couples with a fat member and skinny one, multiracial couples, couples with opposite backgrounds, couples with a mixture of young and old members (especially the cougar-and-cub couple) are all interesting and sometimes considered not likely to have coupled up. Another scenario of the unmatched couple is where the couple's personalities clash, such as the extravert-versus-introvert or the emotional-versus-stoic types. In all these examples, we usually just marvel at how these couples connected (opposites do attract). We wish them well and find their situation interesting at best. The last unlikely couple I will mention is the couple who makes others feel embarrassed for them as a couple. They treat one another so badly that you feel so lucky that you are *not* married to either one of them.

Over the years, my husband and I have met such couples occasionally. My husband and I are quite sociable. We love meeting people. We have been on vacation and met nice couples. Someone would strike up a friendly conversation, and we'd end up dining with complete strangers whom we had met on that very day. We've always had fun and typically enjoyed the company of our new found vacation acquaintances. However, there have been times my husband and I would give one another the eye, signaling that we are so glad not to be married to *that* person. To this day, we sometimes talk about some of the crazy couples we've encountered. I have given nicknames to the women in those relationships. The overall reference is the "wifey" type. Since I am writing from the female perspective, I want to outline a few of the overwhelmingly horrible wifey spouse types whom my husband and I have met over the years and who have caused us to say, "I feel so sorry for her husband." These sad types I have named the bully wife, big mouth wife, wimpy wife, and delusional wife.

The Bully Wife: This lady knows it all; however, she wants her husband to do it all. She has really unreasonable expectations; she is controlling, bossy, disrespectful, and mean. She's the Broomhilda/Cruella de Vil type.

The Big Mouth Wife: She is an excessive complainer who thinks her bad thoughts out loud. She has no filters for word appropriateness. She hardly ever compromises or shows contentment. This woman is not the typical nagging wife. She exemplifies the typical ten times over.

The Wimpy Wife: This woman has no backbone, no creativity, and no excitement; she leaves everything up to her husband and gives him no input or confident feedback. The interesting thing about her is that she is not a shy woman. She avoids conflict; she does all of the I-need-help things—such as tending to the baby, helping with the children's homework, and doing household chores—totally by herself, without help from her spouse. She allows her husband to regard his money as his and her money as his, too.

The Delusional Wife: Everything has to be perfect for this wife. For her, perfect translates to "the right way," or the correct way. She is always by the book. She is unnecessarily detailed about nonessentials. Perfection rules this marriage. Everything must make sense; there is definitely no risk taking and little spontaneity with this woman.

All these wifey types drain the blood, soak up the energy, and suck the air right out of the room. They generally contaminate environments with their bad energy. Everyone feels bad and embarrassed for the husband, and people are afraid that they might hurt his feelings even more if they address his wife's bad behavior.

After reading this section, if you personally identify with any of these ladies, don't feel too bad for too long. It's more important that you stop it and stop behaving badly. You are most likely trying to develop your husband into what you want him to be and what you wish for him to do; you feel this will benefit the marriage. Stop it. Develop yourself. Dig deep, and use that inner strength to *respond, not react.* Respond thoughtfully; don't react emotionally to what you think should be done. We should take care not to make our spouses or ourselves look bad, foolish, or unempowered. We have been created in God's image, and God is not bad, foolish, or unempowered. Just as the woman from Proverbs 31 in the Bible managed to do, use your power to represent God and your husband well. Her husband and those within the city gates spoke well of her: "Her children rise up and call her blessed; Her husband *also,* and he praises her: 'Many daughters have done well, But you excel them all'" (Prov. 31:28–31).

YES, WE CAN, 100 PERCENT

To have a loving, supportive, and encouraging mate is a beautiful expectation. Additionally, loyalty, rationality, and compassion are some character attributes we all want to see in the person we marry. These attributes demonstrate love and respect. I would think people who marry for love want love to continue throughout the entire marriage. What is love? *Webster's Dictionary* has an extensive definition for love. The term "love" has even been defined as a noun and as a verb. No matter how it is used grammatically, the term "love" is really is about value, endearment, and affection. For those in intimate relationships, love includes romance and sexual desire. Who would not wish for love each and every day of one's marriage? Support and encouragement are important aspect of showing love. You need them to show your spouses that you believe in them and their life's purpose. Spousal support and kind words go a long way when nurturing your relationship. Emotions in dysfunctional situations can be diabolic. It is wonderful to rely on a mate who is calm, cool, and tender and who has balanced responses to stressful circumstances.

The intent of equity of effort in a marriage is essential. I don't mean the fifty-fifty theory; I mean each person giving 100 percent toward marital bliss. People who are determined to forgive, love, live, and laugh in their marriages are seemly destined to grow old together. Oh, it's so poetic; every woman wants her man to value her, desire her, whisper sweet nothings to her, and be a strong man of valor devoted to her forever! We women want these things greatly in our relationship. The question is if we give these things in our relationships. Do we have the character attributes that we desire so greatly in our spouses? We can. It is not only up to our spouses to demonstrate this type of love. We can be the very thing that we want our spouses to be. We must live by example. We can't just have these expectations of them. It requires intense effort. It is hard work. We must do our work to have better marriages.

How? How do we give the love we may or may not be getting? We dig deep and use the power of knowledge that "you can do all things through Christ who strengthens you" (Phil. 4:13). I can do all things through Christ who strengthens me.

If you are not a believer in Christ, then understand that others can pray for you! As previously stated, many people believe that the inner power we possess comes from various sources. Find your source. If you need to, lead the way; you will be an example to your mate, and he will follow your lead. Gain the strength, and decide you want to be the best person in your marriage that you can be! If he is already showing you love consistently as you desire, get on board and follow his lead. Mirror his efforts. Glory, Hallelujah. Be in one accord! Give love, and receive love, too. But, please, don't just be a taker!

Love Temperaments: How We Love—*The Five Love Languages* with Dr. Gary Chapman

The previous section of this chapter accentuates using your power to match—even exceed—your spouse's efforts to show love. That section not only espouses using vested power to match the effort of showing love but also gives us tools to show love in the manner that your spouse can receive and appreciate. Both sections address the love demonstration. One talks about the frequency with which mates show love and their good characters. The other looks at what actions you do to show love and whether it is done in the manner that your spouse understands. Having great character traits as a human being is a great start. Using those traits to behave in ways that speak volumes of love to your mate is the goal.

As a workforce-training and professional-development facilitator, I learned years ago of behavioral sciences and the study of personalities.

Although my concentration was tied to personalities in the workplace, I certainly could see that people's personality traits definitely influence their behaviors and expectations of others while they are at work, at home, and at play; they even influence people's interpretations of love. I learned about personality temperaments through various tool assessments, such as the Myers-Briggs Type Indicator, the DISC model, the Strong Interest Inventory profile, and the Holland Code assessment as well as many others.

You might not have heard that there is a theory suggesting the manner of conduct in which people feel loved. Dr. Gary Chapman has written a book called *The Five Love Languages: The Secret to Love That Lasts.* In this book, he outlines the five different ways people express love, or need love shown to them, in order to feel valued, appreciated, and desirable: *loved.* Dr. Chapman outlines these languages as

Words of Affirmation
Actions don't always speak louder than words. If this is your love language, unsolicited compliments mean the world to you. Hearing the words "I love you" is important—hearing the reasons behind that love sends your spirits skyward. Insults can leave you shattered and are not easily forgotten.

Quality Time
For those whose love language is spoken with Quality Time, nothing says "I love you" like full, undivided attention. Being there for this type of person is critical, but really being there— with the TV off, fork and knife down, and all chores and tasks on standby—makes your significant other feel truly special and loved. Distractions, postponed dates, or the failure to listen can be especially hurtful.

Receiving Gifts
Don't mistake this love language for materialism; the receiver of gifts thrives on the love, thoughtfulness, and effort behind

the gift. If you speak this language, the perfect gift or gesture shows that you are known, you are cared for, and you are prized above whatever was sacrificed to bring the gift to you. A missed birthday, anniversary, or a hasty, thoughtless gift would be disastrous—so would the absence of everyday gestures.

Acts of Service

Can vacuuming the floors really be an expression of love? Absolutely! Anything you do to ease the burden of responsibilities weighing on an "Acts-of-Service" person will speak volumes. The words he or she most want to hear: "Let me do that for you." Laziness, broken commitments, and making more work for them tell speakers of this language their feelings don't matter.

Physical Touch

This language isn't all about the bedroom. A person whose primary language is Physical Touch is, not surprisingly, very touchy. Hugs, pats on the back, holding hands, and thoughtful touches on the arm, shoulder, or face—they can all be ways to show excitement, concern, care, and love. Physical presence and accessibility are crucial, while neglect or abuse can be unforgivable and destructive.

It is most important to consider the needs of our spouses. It is imperative if you want peace, love, and happiness in your marriage. This means to respond positively to whatever language of love your spouse speaks. I point out Dr. Chapman's work as a tool to share with you that shows you how to demonstrate love to your spouses according to their barometers. Use your vested power to restrain from selfishness, laziness, and inconsideration. Use your strength to give your spouses what they need, on their terms and without conviction. That means no complaining. Like Nike states, "Just do it." You can. You have the will and inner strength to do so.

What's at stake here? Consider your options; if you want a better marriage, dig deep and pull up that strength of sacrifice and compromise for those things that are for the good of the marriage. Use your gifts faithfully, and they shall be enlarged; practice what you know, and you shall attain a higher knowledge. What's the point in having an inner strength or power and not using it? It is no secret we have such a thing. So why not use it? What if Superman refused to fly, or Spiderman refused to use his Spidey senses? While bullets were flying her way, what if Wonder Woman hadn't used those bullet-deflecting wrist cuffs she wore? Do you understand where I am going with this? It doesn't make sense to let useful power lay dormant.

I encourage you to use your gifts, use your strengths, and use your inner power to ensure dreamy love, blissful companionship, great future, and lifelong good sex.

In conclusion, I must express that I am so proud to be a part of this book project. I have been married for over twenty years. This experience of sharing with my friends, the coauthors of this resource tool, has been phenomenal. Over the span of my twenty-year marriage, I have learned some techniques to stay married, to stay sane, and to stay confident that marriages evolve and successes are possible. Uniting with other women to encourage and share war stories in a loving, nonjudgmental, and constructive way has been tremendously rewarding. The number of years these women have been married ranges from six years to twenty-plus years. Believe it or not, even with my many years of marriage, this experience of writing with others about marriage has been a transformative experience for me. In regard to problems in my marriage, I have learned to consistently live what God gave me.

Consistent use of vested power is now my marriage mantra. By faith, I've known about inner strength of power for years. I would dig deep sometimes to use it, and other times I would be the typical nagging wife. However, I refused to be the obnoxious complaining wifey. I was only using my power partially, sparingly. To return to the electricity analogy, there is no need to conserve good strength. I was basically sitting in the dark and sulking—even worse, stumbling around—in the dark while the power generator was on. I simply would not turn on the light switch. Sitting in the heat when you need cool air or sitting in the dark when you need light is just not wise.

As a result of being a part of this book-writing cohort, I have reconnected with my personal belief of using inner strength and power. While I was writing my chapter in this book, my marriage went haywire; we went through some unexpected emotional hardships and experienced the types of emotions that newlyweds, not twenty-year veterans, might have. They didn't happen because of my involvement in writing the book. No, my husband agreed to my involvement and was aware of my subject matter. I believe God allowed the circumstances contributing to our frustrations to show me the value and significance of His principle of vested power. By using the power vested in me, I dug deep to understand what I needed to do to keep peace and harmony in my life. I dug deep to understand this principle, and I even adjusted my communication style to collaborate better with my husband.

Consequently, he and I began to talk more. We had already talked, but now our talks were deep! We talked about who our married selves had become and what it meant for our future. We peeled back layers of misunderstandings. We uncovered that when we married, we had been two imperfect vessels joining our imperfections together. We had major good qualities, yes, but the bad ones were wreaking havoc. The bad ones had lain dormant; we had never really worked on them. We ignored them because we loved each other. Keep in mind that even though your spouse doesn't say much about your bad flaws, you should still work on them. Don't let those little pesky goblins grow up to be big, bad, out-of-control monsters.

We were two imperfect—some might say broken—vessels, who had never really worked on helping each other become God's idea of being whole. We had really never helped each other be God's best. We were trying to be "one," united as one, but we were so broken—not broken in half but broken into pieces. We were not making a complete whole. We needed God to fill in our broken spots so that we could eventually get to the whole in our marriage. As a result of my experience writing this chapter, I learned to use vested power to aid us in agreeing to help each other be God's whole. For twenty years, it had been like trying to put puzzle pieces together to complete the puzzle, but the pieces were tattered, torn, wiggly, or frayed. You can see what the puzzle is supposed to be, but it looks so raggedy! It's put together, but it's a mess! That's what we were until we understood the benefit of using the vested power. To date, we have allowed God to tape, glue, re-cut, and fix up the puzzle pieces. We look brand-new.

My objective for participating with my friends on this project is the hope that people reading this book will, themselves, be inspired or will encourage someone else to always work on staying together in marriage (excluding abandoned or abusive marriages). I have personally resolved for myself that if I use the inner strength that God has bestowed in a good way, I may never have to endure the experience of a judge pronouncing my marriage to be legally dissolved. As a deterrent to that experience, I'm committed to using vested power for the good of my marriage. How about you?

SELF-REFLECTION QUESTIONS

What is your love language?

_____

_____

_____

_____

_____

_____

What is your spouse's love language?

_____

_____

_____

_____

_____

How will you use your vested power?

_____

_____

_____

_____

_____

CHAPTER 2

LORD, IS THIS MY ISSUE OR OUR ISSUE?

Marriages are threatened when we try to make our issue
our mate's issue. Discover the power in holding your
peace and letting the Lord fight your battles.

THEME: TRUST AND PATIENCE

When I first got married, I remember someone asking me, "How does it feel now that you are married?" Instead of radiating the essence of marital bliss and romanticized love, I remember saying, "I feel stuck." The person with whom I was speaking rightly responded with a "huh," and I explained further. What I realized I was saying was that now that I was married, I no longer had the easy option of kicking my husband out of my apartment whenever we had a disagreement. I could not "send him to his room," as if he were a child; I had to put in the hard work or effort needed to work it out, as marriage requires.

When issues arise in my marriage, I have learned to ask, "God, is this *my* issue or *our* issue?" I go on to ask, "Lord, if it is *my* issue, help me to deal with me. If it is *our* issue, Lord, do you want me to say something?" Incidentally, He always tells me no. He reminds me that He is in control and not me. Oftentimes in our marriages, we tend to create issues where there are no issues. We tend to make our own issues our spouse's issues and, therefore, create havoc in the marriage. We forget that although we are one in marriage, we are two individuals with two different histories, two different personalities, and two different upbringings. The "one flesh" (Gen. 2:24) that God calls us to in marriage requires effort, commitment, acknowledgment, forgiveness, and love of a lifetime: a God kind of love.

Any person who has been married for any length of time can tell you that being in a marriage relationship takes *effort*, something done by exertion or hard work. A good marriage does not happen on its own; it needs two people willing to put in the hard work that it takes to create a harmonious union. You are no longer a single unit living alone but a double unit becoming one. It is no longer "me" and "mine"; it is "us" and "ours."

Next is *commitment*, which is the promise or obligation made during the wedding ceremony through the vow in which you promised your "lawfully wedded spouse, to have and to hold, from this day forward, for better, for worse, for richer, for poorer, in sickness and in health, until death do us part" (or some other similar statement). There was not a caveat or condition to bail when things got tough—especially, and not exclusively, for Christians. This commitment was made before God and to God, which implies that we have to trust that God can handle our difficult times. One way in which we demonstrate the commitment to our marriages is through our ability to acknowledge our differences. We must *acknowledge* that our way is not the only way and not necessarily the right way. Just because your mother did it this way does not mean that the way that your spouse's mother did it was wrong; it could just be one of your own pet peeves. A pet peeve is a minor annoyance that people identify as particularly annoying to themselves.

For me, I have several pet peeves that, if not acknowledged and contained, can make mountains out of molehills. One of those pet peeves is people not cleaning up the kitchen after themselves, in particular, not cleaning up or wiping down the counters when they are through. Unfortunately, this is not an issue for my husband, who oftentimes makes sandwiches on the counter and leaves the bread crumbs on the counter *after* I have cleaned it. As for me, prior to putting a sandwich together, I typically take out all of the items that I will use; this includes a plate or napkin for the bread and the cutting board for the tomatoes, onions, and so on. With the bread on the plate or napkin, I begin to make my sandwich. I use the cutting board to cut the tomatoes and onions, and I clean up after myself afterward, leaving no crumbs or mess behind. My husband, on the other hand, puts the bread directly on the counter—no plate, no napkin. Ugh! When his sandwich is made, he nonchalantly picks it up from the counter, crumbs remaining, and walks, sandwich in tow, to the table or to another room in the house—with *no* napkin; and me, I look at the counter in disgust because he has left crumbs on what used to be my clean countertop. In my mind, it looks like the scene in the movie *The Color Purple* where Danny Glover's character, Mister, puts his muddy, dirty, boots on the table that his wife Celie has just cleaned. Of course, that is an exaggeration. Leaving crumbs on the counter and putting muddy boots on the table are clearly not the same; but as I said previously, in my mind that is how I saw it, and thus, I created a mountain out of a molehill.

I used to make a big deal out of it by telling him to clean up the crumbs or by getting a napkin for him to wrap the sandwich in while he walked around. When that did not work, I would get a plate and put the bread on the plate before he began making it, would slip a napkin under the bread, or would just get sassy and sound off about his lack of home training. Needless to say, this molehill became a mountain because I had tried to make my own issue my husband's issue. One day while I was sharing this story at a married-couple's retreat, one of the women commented that at least I kept the counter clean enough for him to put his bread on. You could have knocked me over with a feather; I had never thought about it in that way. That simple yet profound statement hit a nerve and challenged me to reflect on where my feelings about the "crumbs on the counter" came from—on what was really going on.

As I did some self-refection, I realized that those feelings came from a place in my own upbringing and environment where living in public housing oftentimes resulted in a pest-control problem. I could not stand them then and cannot stand them now, and I sure did not want bugs to be a part of my current living conditions. The choice to do some self-reflection helped me to confront the truth of my frustration and to learn to identify and acknowledge my own issue. If you do not acknowledge your own shortcoming(s), you cannot confront them. If you do not confront them, you cannot resolve them. Acknowledging my own shortcomings allowed me to be more compassionate and forgiving of my husband and to get over myself. The *World English Dictionary* defines forgiveness as the ability to cease to blame or hold resentment against someone or something. In marriage, we have to learn to forgive a whole lot of stuff; we have to let some things go. If I had not learned to see the bread crumbs on the counter for what they were (a man making a sandwich), I would have put undue strain on my marriage. The ability and willingness to forgive is a necessity in marriage because unforgiveness is a virus that will slowly infect your marriage and tear it to shreds. Our ability and willingness to forgive are so hard because true forgiveness leaves us vulnerable, exposed, and transparent. The transparency manifested by the two people in the marriage requires that we learn to trust God in this space.

TRUSTING GOD IN THIS SPACE

The Bible says, "Trust in the Lord with all thine heart and lean not on to your own understanding. In all thy ways acknowledge Him and He will direct thy paths" (Prov. 3:5–6) and "The Lord is my shepherd, I shall not want" (Ps. 23:1). But how can I pray the Lord's Prayer when my heart is heavy and my mind is clouded? How can I pray "the Lord is my shepherd, I shall not want" when the wants for my marriage are many?

- I want to be a godly wife, the one who "gets up while it is still night and provides food for her family" and whose husband and children call her blessed (Prov. 31:15, 28). I want to be that woman without consideration of fleshly and conditional thoughts of "but what about him."
- I want to submit the headship of my marriage to my husband (Eph. 5:22–4) and be released from the independent spirit that oftentimes invades my space.
- I want to walk "in the grace and knowledge of our Lord and Savior Jesus Christ (2 Pet. 3:18), the grace of God being that unearned and undeserved favor. By grace, I want to pass this unearned and undeserved favor to my husband "For the grace given to me" (Rom. 12:3).
- I want to stand and "see the salvation of the Lord" (Exod. 14:3). I want to stand in the truth that God can do anything but fail. He can heal the hurts of marriage and deliver me into a new space of trust.
- I want "the peace of God that surpasses all understanding" (Phil. 4:7). I know that peace can only come when I learn to fully rely on God.

- I want a love that "is patient and kind" (1 Cor. 13:4), not one that is easily frustrated when things don't go my way.

The wants of our marriages can become reality when we have the courage to submit our own will to the will of God. This means leaving our familiar places—those places of comfort, control, and competence—to go to a place of vulnerability, a place where we are exposed, susceptible, and in a weakened position. By choosing to marry, we also choose vulnerability. In this vulnerable place, the complexity of marriage evolves. It evolves from our familiar places into the great mystery of marriage referenced in Ephesians: "For this reason a man shall leave his father and mother and be joined to his wife, and the two shall become one flesh. This is a great mystery, but I speak concerning Christ and the church" (Eph. 5:31–2).

Recognizing Your Familiar Place

Familiar places are the customary, habitual, usual, recurring, typical, recognizable, traditional, and unconstrained responses or reactions we resort to when things do not go our way or when things get tough, especially in the marriage relationship. Many of these familiar places are part of the baggage that we bring into the marriage: things that our mothers told us; things that our daddy showed us; or just old information that we have obtained from some well-meaning "barracks lawyers." (A "barracks lawyer" is an old military term used to describe people who know a whole lot about nothing and who have an opinion, answer, or solution to everything. I'll talk about them a little later.) In order to navigate through the complexities of marriage, we must acknowledge our own familiar places, their origins, and the impact that they have on our marital relationships. Some of the "baggage" brought into my marriage was based on faulty counsel received from all of the aforementioned sources.

My mother was a great woman who imparted great wisdom into my life. In addition to being the person who introduced me to the church, she was an excellent cook. She was also a woman of her times, meaning that she believed that the husband was responsible for being the sole provider of the family, which my dad was. When we kids were all in school, she went to work and began making her own money. I don't remember what prompted the conversation, but she used to tell us girls, "A man does not need to know how much you make. Your money is your money; his money is for the family." Not only is that not scriptural, it is just plain selfish. However, this mentality impacted my early relationships and was brought into my marriage. My expectation was that a man must make enough money to provide for all of the needs and wants of the family even though I have been working all of my adult life and making a pretty decent salary.

Before I was married, I placed limits on the amount of money that I would spend on a man or boyfriend; the maximum amount that I would spend on a gift was $25, and that was only if I had been in a relationship for at least six months. (You can bet that I didn't have a lot of long relationships.) My mind-set was that I was not going to let a man "rip me off" or not hold up to his "responsibility" of being the sole provider. Needless to say, all of these crazy ideas relating to money were brought into my marriage. We had separate accounts during the early years of my marriage and have since combined our accounts. Even now, money and financial stewardship can be a point of contention in my marriage. I always have to remember that "God is the source of my strength" (Ps. 59:9), He is Jehovah Jireh, my provider (Gen. 22:14) and that "I have never seen the righteous forsaken or their children begging bread" (Ps. 37:25). Knowing this also reduces the stress in my marriage and allows God to be God and not me.

Some other baggage brought into my marriage came from my father, as he was the example for and standard to which I held all men. My dad knew how to clean the house and made sure that all of the children (my brother and sisters) knew how to scrub and wax the floors, clean the bathrooms, polish the brass, and so on. (I am sure that his navy service had something to do with this.) He was also a great cook, prepared outstanding meals from scratch, and ensured that we cleaned the kitchen afterward. (As I'm writing this part, the "bread-crumbs-on-the-counter" situation has come to mind; could this be a manifestation of my dad's influence?) He always worked hard and made sure that his family was taken care of. I'm not saying that he was perfect because he was not, but he is a great dad and set a great standard.

The last sort of baggage brought into my marriage came from the faulty logic of the "barracks lawyers." This familiar place can be easily identified by the way that statements are framed. They typically begin with "Girl, if I were you, I would" and "Girl, I wouldn't let him talk to me like that" or with other similar statements. We need to be particularly mindful of the counsel that we seek when it comes to our marriages. The Word reminds us to "Consider the outcome of their way of life and imitate their faith" (Heb. 13:7). Just because a person is a Christian does not mean that he or she will always provide godly counsel. As the scripture says, "Consider the outcome of their way of life and imitate their faith" (Heb. 13:7). Is their marriage one that glorifies God? Do they speak faith or flesh into your situation? Do they encourage you to be still and know that He is God (Ps. 46:10). Or do they promote your eagerness to sabotage your marriage, to disrespect your spouse, and to tear your house down? These are important factors to consider when seeking counsel regarding your marriage. Proverbs says, "The wise woman builds her house, but with her own hands the foolish one tears hers down" (Prov. 14:1).

For me, I seek strength in the Word. However, there are times when I need to share my feelings with another married Christian sister, and fortunately there are a handful of people with whom God has blessed me and with whom I can be completely transparent and honest as it relates to growing in marriage. Nevertheless, in order to navigate through the intricacies of marriage, we must acknowledge our own familiar places, their origins, and the impact that they have on our marital relationships.

How do you respond when your spouse says or does something that offends you or hurts your feelings? What is your familiar place?

- Do you retaliate with similar actions?
- Do you shut down and give your spouse the silent treatment?
- Do you walk out, ignore the situation, and hang out with friends?
- Do you play the "I'm-grown" card and do what you want to do?
- Do you call out to God the Father?

These are some of the responses or reactions we resort to when things don't go our way or when things get tough. Oftentimes, when I am teaching a Bible study or other class and the subject of marriage or relationship ensues, someone, almost without fail, will ask the question, "Why am I the one who always has to apologize when he was the one who hurt me or who was wrong?" My response is always the same: "You are the one to apologize because your heart is the one that is ready for change; it is the one that is being convicted." Just know that your heart can change for the better or for the worse. Also, know that you are not apologizing for his actions but for your part in the fight or argument. When God replaced your heart of stone with a heart of flesh (Ezek. 11:19), that heart transplant also brought with it the capacity to feel—flesh feels things. The same heart that feels love also cracks when it breaks. That same heart that laughs also cries. That same heart that cares is also scared. Nevertheless, we must be willing to seek a new familiar place in Christ. I admit that this is very hard to do; in fact, it is impossible to do without God. Yet, as the scripture says, "with man this is impossible, but with God all things are possible" (Matt. 19:26).

Finding Your Familiar Place in Christ

Just like we know our own bodies—its aches and pains, likes and dislikes—becoming one with our spouses means recognizing, understanding, and knowing their nuances. What makes them smile? What hurts their feelings? What are they allergic to? This, of course, has to be intentional because it takes effort. It takes effort because it is not our natural or familiar place. Things that are familiar to us are habitual, usual, recurring, typical, or recognizable; we know what they look like and feel like. On the other hand, things that are not familiar to us feel strange or unnatural because they are foreign, new, strange, uncommon, undistinguished, unfamiliar, and unknown. Nonetheless, we have to find our familiar place in Christ and ask, "What would Jesus do?" I know that this is not always practical or comfortable, but, trust me, it is dependable.

When things in my marriage are strained and I am challenged to deal with it, my flesh would have me to respond in a way that would make me feel better and would make my spouse feel my pain; however, my spirit says no. As I strive to become a stronger woman of faith, I must continually remain in prayer and consider what would Jesus do—if consulting the Father was good enough for Him, then it is, sure enough, good enough for me. As I choose to remain married to this man, I must dare to love him.

DARING TO LOVE

How many times during your youth (or now) did you make a dare? How many times did you challenge someone with the words "I dare you to"? A dare is a challenge made to another person to prove his or her courage, usually through taking a risk. There are many things that I remember doing as a child as a result of accepting a dare; they all led to negative consequences. However, daring to love your spouse does not have to result in a negative consequence. Do you have the courage to accept the risk of loving him? I dare you.

As a young girl, I remember dreaming about marriage in the fantasized, romanticized, prince-charming-coming-to-scoop-me-up kind of way—filled with carriages, gowns, food, family, friends, honeymoons, and so on—only to enter into the reality of planning a marriage that was more in line with what we could afford. When I dreamed of marriage as a child, I did not attach any cost to my fantasies; because in "fantasy island", all things just are. Now, twenty-three years later, my marriage has weathered all sorts of challenges—highs and lows, excitements and disappointments, celebrations and snubs—yet through it all, I have decided to incorporate strategies within my marriage that will help to keep it strong.

One such strategy is what I call my "marriage key ring." A key ring is an apparatus designed to hold the keys that an individual needs to access something that is locked or to lock something that is opened, such as a car, a door, or a heart. Each marriage should build a key ring consisting of a variety of keys used to open or unlock the heart of each mate and contribute to a successful marriage. Some of the keys on my marriage key ring include the following.

Humor. Couples should find something that they both find funny, even when it seems that they are the only two people in the world who get the joke. As the two of you progress in becoming one flesh, you begin to see things the same; the experiences you have shared now become points of humor between you since the two of you have a uniquely shared experience. My husband and I have several things that we now see as funny even though they are corny to everyone else. One example I can share is from the movie *Money Talks*, starring Chris Tucker and Charlie Sheen. Chris Tucker is a man on the run from the police and is trying to clear his name in a murder case. Charlie Sheen is a news reporter who has elected to hide or cover for Chris Tucker in hopes of getting the exclusive story. As Chris is hanging out with Charlie, who is also getting married and needs to attend his wedding rehearsal, Charlie tells Chris that he needs to hang out with him and pretend to be a college friend. Chris has no clothes and must wear one of Charlie's suits. Chris, of course, chooses the best suit and is admiring himself in the mirror; Charlie notices the suit and comments on Chris's choice of the suit. Chris states that Charlie is jealous because he looks better in the suit than Charlie does; in fact, he says that he looks like the "Ebony Man of the Month," a feature in *Ebony* magazine. Charlie is so frustrated and running late that he does not have time to argue with Chris or to make him change clothes, and they head to the wedding rehearsal. Now every time my husband gets dressed up and is checking himself out in the mirror, I will refer to him as the Ebony Man of the Month, and he sometimes will refer to himself as the Ebony Man of the Month when he believes that he is looking good. Again, this is something that an outsider would not think of as funny but the two of us do. There are several other examples I could give, but I believe the point is made. Learn to laugh at yourselves and with yourselves.

Compliments. Several years ago, James Ingram had a hit song called "Find One Hundred Ways." The song began with the following words: "Compliment what she does, send her roses just because. If it's violins she loves, let them play. Dedicate her favorite song and hold her closer all night long. Love her today, find one hundred ways." Complimenting my husband is a key that I have recently added to my key ring as a means for not taking him for granted. He is an awesome cook and griller and enjoys cooking for me. He also likes to know that I enjoy what he has taken the time to prepare, so he will ask me what I think. If I am at the house while he is cooking, he will bring me samples of the food to taste, such as a piece of a steak that he has grilled or a forkful of creamed spinach that he has whipped up. He will then stare at me while I chew the food to observe my reaction. If it is the steak, he will say something like "It tastes like butter, doesn't it?" Most of the time it does "taste like butter," and I will tell him so; however, I oftentimes will look around the kitchen to see what a mess he's made and break the rhythm by complaining about the kitchen. (Here I go again.) All of his efforts to please me are canceled out by my concern with the mess. Does this sound familiar?

Because I am now aware of my how my actions affect my husband and, thus, my marriage, I am learning to stop sweating the small stuff and learning to stop to smell the roses. Instead of complaining about the mess that he's made, I become an active partner in the activity and clean the kitchen—whether I was at home during the preparation or whether I walked in and it was already done. One of the best things that

I have learned to do is to "find one hundred ways" to love my husband, which includes complimenting him. Besides, the payoff is tremendous.

Prayer. In our marriages, God often allows us to see things in and about our spouses that no one else has access to and vice versa. Our spouses are given the privilege of seeing us at our best and at our worse; no one else in the world has been given or blessed with such a unique vantage point. I refer to these vantage points as unique prayer opportunities. Something that is unique exists as the only one or the sole example. In this particular case, a unique prayer opportunity means that God has given you access to something that no one else has seen in exactly the same way that you have been exposed to it. You have been given a unique and special opportunity to pray for someone or something in a way opened to you solely by God. Pray for those things exposed to you by God. Instead of calling your in-laws, girlfriends, or male friends or just plain ol' nagging, I challenge you to just pray. Ephesians says, "And pray in the Spirit on all occasions with all kinds of prayers and requests. With this in mind, praying for all the saints" (Eph. 6:18). This includes your husband even if he is not a saint.

Trust. Proverbs tells us to "Trust in the LORD with all your heart, And lean not on your own understanding; In all your ways acknowledge Him, And He shall direct your paths" (Prov. 3:5–6). This passage has been a source of support for me as I journey through marriage. I have found that I have to trust in the Lord with *all* my heart and not some of it. As previously mentioned, God has removed my heart of stone and has changed it to heart of flesh (Ezek. 36:26). A heart of flesh feels; that same heart that loves also hurts. When my heart has been broken and my feeling heart wants to lash out in anger, I take it to God. When I don't want to trust again, I take it to God. When I don't want to be married anymore, I take it to God. As the opening scripture says, lean not on to your own understanding; trust God. My own understanding would have me "get to the bottom of it." My own understanding would have me pack up and leave. My own understanding would have me give in and give up—but for God. As the old spiritual song goes, "I will trust in the

Lord, I will trust in the Lord, I will trust in the Lord, until I die." I now understand a little better why they repeated the phrases; it was to get it into our spirits, to repeat it until it becomes our reality. I will trust in the Lord until I die. Hallelujah!

Faith. The Bible says, "Now, faith is the substance of things hoped for, the evidence of things not seen" (Heb. 11:1). The *Oxford University Dictionary* defines substance as "the real physical matter of which a person or thing consists and which has a tangible, solid presence." What real physical, tangible, and solid presence are you hoping for in your marriage relationship? Are you hoping for physical, solid evidence of a change in your spouse? Are you hoping for physical, solid evidence of a change in yourself? Are you looking for evidence, manifested in a tangible, solid presence, to an unanswered prayer? Well, so am I. Marriage is a walk of faith that we enter into, hopeful of the substance that is to come—a house to make a home, children to expand the family, and a mate to love forever. As we live in it, we look for the evidence of the yet-unseen things and sometimes lose hope that the substance will manifest into that physical, solid, evidence. While we wait, remember that God is able do exceedingly abundantly above all that we ask or think (Eph. 3:20).

Finally, because I have chosen to marry, I have chosen to love. I have chosen not a selfish kind love that relies on feelings, emotions, and conditions but a God kind of love that fully relies on God. This kind of love is an agape love, a rare kind of love demonstrated by God, which should be the mission of our marriages. After the vows and the celebration festivities comes the work of loving and cherishing my spouse from this day forward.

In closing, I must say that I have been truly blessed and honored to be a part of this book project. This group of women whom God has called together "for such a time as this" (Esther 4:14) is truly special; these women have prayed, encouraged, and laughed with me throughout. I pray that God will do the same for you. Many blessings.

SELF-REFLECTION QUESTIONS

Have you ever tried to make your issue your spouse's issue? How has this impacted your marriage?

_____

_____

_____

_____

_____

Do you have a familiar place that you resort to when your spouse hurts your feelings? Have you discovered the origin of your reaction?

_____

_____

_____

_____

_____

What are some other keys that you can add to your marriage key ring?

_____

_____

_____

_____

_____

CHAPTER 3

WILL YOU LOVE HIM?

At a time in my marriage when I felt the sting of
deception, the stench of regret, and the anxiety of
rejection, Jesus asked me, "Will you love Him?" Unlike
Peter, I did not immediately answer. I was shocked
by the question, so He asked me again, "Will you
love Him?"

THEME: LOVE AND TRUST

The third time He said to him, "Simon (Peter) son of John, do
you love me?" Peter was hurt because Jesus asked him the third
time, "Do you love me?" He said, "Lord, you know all things;
you know that I love you." Jesus said, "Feed my sheep."

—JOHN 21:17

AT A TIME in my marriage when I felt the sting of deception, the stench of regret, and the anxiety of rejection, Jesus asked me, "Will you love Him?" Unlike Peter, I did not immediately answer. I was shocked by the question, so He asked me again, "Will you Love Him?" I still couldn't answer. I knew what I wanted to say, but my hurt and anger would not release me. The third time Jesus asked me "Will you love Him?" my answer was yes, and it still is.

I believe that, just as he had asked Peter, Jesus was asking me whether or not I was ready to give up what I wanted, what I envisioned for myself, and what I felt I deserved. He was asking me whether I was ready to give up the image of marriage and commitment that I had painted in my own mind for His love, His honesty with me, His commitment to me, and His acceptance of me. That was deep. And I said, "Yes, but."

There are no buts.

THE STING OF DECEPTION

Whitney Houston told me that "I'm every woman" and that my husband is "All the man that I'll need." If that's the case, why am I reading this e-mail, this encrypted yet somehow-blaringly clear message that she had told me wrong?

What do you do when you realize another woman has your husband's attention, is taking some of his time, is making him feel desirable somehow, and is feeding some psyche that you didn't even know was starved? Even more difficult, how do you respond when his reaction to your concern over this communication is merely that nothing is going on?

You already answered the question in your mind, didn't you? You check his e-mail, his cell phone, his mail, his pockets, and his nightstand. You monitor his phone calls and ask, "Who was that?" Now, of course, you know that I didn't do any of those things, right?

You become suspicious, angry, and, in the worst case, spiteful and mean. How long do I want to live like this? I had to finally ask myself. He was fine; he had moved on, apologized, and said it wouldn't happen again, and I was still stuck. Stuck in the moment that I first saw the message. Stuck in a television rerun where I got to replay the scene: how I reacted, what I shoulda said, what I'll say next time.

This is when Jesus first asked me, "Will you love Him?" I didn't answer. I was still angry. I was still hurt. I was still reliving the unbelievable horror that my husband had hurt me—as if I had thought he never would. That is what I thought, didn't I? That was my idea of marriage and commitment: two people who loved each other unconditionally, insatiably, and so much that they would never do anything to hurt each other. How realistic was that?

So now I had to stop focusing on him and start asking myself some questions. The first was the most obvious: Did I really believe that I would marry this man and be with him forever, ever and that he would never hurt me? Since I knew that the mere reality of that wasn't even feasible, the answer was no. The next question wasn't so obvious, but it was the hardest one of all: OK, since you knew that, what did you plan to do when you got hurt? Were you planning to leave? Planning to stay? Planning to make him pay for it for the rest of the marriage?

Where were Cinderella and the happily ever after when you needed them? The chapter left out of that story was playing out in my life, and I had decisions to make. Those decisions had everything to do with *me*: how I handle my disappointments and how I handle my marriage. So, instead of answering Jesus's question to me, I asked Him one: Why is this happening to me? Over the course of the next few years, He showed me.

THE STENCH OF REGRET

I was doing everything right, by the book; I was a good wife, so I felt. Why would any man worth having mess that up? I wasn't going to take it; I didn't have to (I know you've said that one), and I'm gonna…I'll let you fill in the blanks.

Are you familiar with the saying "Throw the rock; hide the hand"? This saying describes the actions of someone who has committed an action only to feel ashamed, fearful, or regretful. We all do and say things that we sometimes regret. In a marriage, regret is not just a six-letter word; it's a divisive, reclusive, and paralyzing word.

I hurt you, so you hurt me; and then we both regret what we said or did. We say we are sorry; or, even worse, we don't, and the dark cloud remains. The only thing that can break through the stench is forgiveness. Yes, I said the "f" word. Forgiveness? Forgive whom? Him? After what he did? You know how it plays out in our heads: "He's not getting off that easy…He just can't treat me any kind of way and think…I'm a grown-ass woman, and I don't have to…" Again, I'll let you fill in the blanks.

Without forgiveness, regret takes on a life of its own. Yes, let's be honest: a little remorse can initially bring some flowers, some jewelry, or some desired attention, but lingering remorse, unforgiven, turns to shame. This shame builds walls between you and your spouse. If you were walking around your spouse constantly believing that he was judging you because of some past wrongdoing or just waiting for you to mess up so that he could remind you of how he knew you would mess up, you would begin to emotionally shut down in the relationship. God showed me how my marriage was heading into shutdown mode.

I decided that I did not want my biggest regret to be unforgiveness and the resultant loss of a marriage that I knew, right down in the heart of it, that I truly wanted. Man, this stuff is hard.

THE ANXIETY OF REJECTION

I brought baggage to my marriage. My baggage included being in a long-term relationship where I was lied to, cheated on, and made to feel unsuitable. I had grown up in a loving nuclear family, but I had always felt somewhat outcast and rejected by my very blended and extended family. I had few friends and often felt that I didn't fit in; truth be told, I still feel that way sometimes. More simply, I brought acceptance issues to my marriage. That deep-down insecure place crept up in my marriage whenever I felt my husband's actions were a rejection of me. Of course, he had no idea about my old wound, and he didn't know that the emotion I exhibited when I was hurt or disappointed was a compilation of a history he knew nothing about.

It took me years to recognize the connection. Why did I get my feelings hurt so easily? Why would I get so angry when he didn't like what I liked or didn't want to do what I wanted? In the early years of my marriage, I often prayed and asked God to "fix" my husband: "Lord, help him." Eventually, God answered me by revealing a stronghold in my life that was plaguing me.

Why me? It's a question people often ask themselves when they are seeking understanding or explanation for some unpleasant event in their lives. I asked myself this question: Why would a man who had a woman who loved him unconditionally, who would do anything for him, who supports him and encourages him, and who works hard to be a good mother and dutiful wife do anything that would threaten his marriage? Why would he risk losing a good thing, the one he loves? Maybe he's unhappy. Maybe he loves someone else. Maybe I'm not what he really wants. Maybe, maybe, maybe. And the anxiety kicks in.

I wasn't just feeling the rejection in my marriage, but all the feelings of inadequacy and rejection I often felt growing up snowballed and were dragged up: "I just don't fit in; I'm not the popular or first choice." The baggage in my life was getting bigger and heavier. At first, I didn't even recognize the fact that I was carrying it, and when it got overwhelming, I'd go to God. Through tears I would ask Him to help me. I was tired of feeling inadequate. I was tired of trying to fit in. For the first time, I asked Him not for others' acceptance of me but for my acceptance of myself. I realized that I had internalized so many of these feelings that I had always counted myself out before anyone else did. I always felt inadequate even if no one was treating me that way. I expected rejection. Until I accepted me, no one else could. So I asked God to please help me to learn to accept myself—all of me.

I was in my own way. From outward appearances, no one would have guessed or understood it. I had all the attributes and possessions of what many define as a successful person, but I was broken. I whipped out some old self-esteem techniques that I had used in high school; I looked in the mirror and said positive affirming things about myself. I began taking inventory of my accomplishments, the friendships I had made, and the community work I had done. I looked at the success of my children and the home I had made for them to thrive in. I was valuable. I was needed. I was respected. I was wanted.

The Bible says, "I praise you because I am fearfully and wonderfully made; your works are wonderful, I know that full well" (Ps. 139:14). "More than a conqueror," "God's workmanship," and "a child of God": these were all words I had heard and even stated before, but it wasn't until I had internalized what those words were saying about me—about who I was and who I had the potential to become—that I gained the strength and the confidence to answer in a resounding yes when God asked me again, "Will you love him?"

I had to love myself enough to know that no matter how much someone else does or does not love me, it doesn't change who I am. I had to love myself enough to know that someone else's attitudes, behaviors, and opinions don't define who I am—even if that someone else is my spouse.

I love him. That doesn't mean he'll never hurt me, never disappoint me, never disrespect me, never fail me, or never stop loving me. What I had to learn was how to love in those times when I wasn't feeling equally loved in return. I had to define my response to hurts and disappointment before they happened so that I would be equipped to manage those moments and not let emotions drive my words and actions.

His Honesty with Me

I spent the better portion of my life trying to fit in, trying to feel accepted, and needing to feel wanted. It wasn't until I truly began to grow spiritually that I understood that God had already accepted me, had always wanted me, and, in His infinite plan, needs me to be obedient in order to fulfill His work in me. It wasn't until then that I realized that it was unrealistic and, in many ways, selfish to expect that my husband would like or agree with everything I did or said. Again, God asked me, "Will you love him?" I had to ask God to forgive me for my selfishness and to heal me from my brokenness. I am a work in progress. "A work in progress" means that I'm still working on it. Just because I have come to realize the source of my insecurity and just because I have decided to love my husband unconditionally doesn't mean that I don't still experience the feelings of rejection or hurt. It means that I'm better equipped to recognize those emotions, put them into perspective, and not use them as the foundation upon which my marriage relies.

The amazing part of this journey is that I realize that I started by asking God to "fix him" and now know that, in order for me to be the wife that God has called me to be, God must "fix me." Fix my heart; fix my mind; fix my attitude; and fix my outlook.

A quote, whose author is unknown, was recently shared with me on a social media site, and it resonates with me for so many reasons. The quote states, "A marriage is two imperfect people who refuse to give up on each other." The words "imperfect" and "refuse" make this quote immensely profound. Isn't this how God loves us? We are imperfect. He knows we are, but He refuses to give up on us because He loves us. Instead, He shows us love and gives us grace and mercy. God was being honest and clear with me. How could I desire and expect this from Him but refuse to bestow it on my husband? Will you love him?

If I could read your mind, you might be thinking, "I'm no doormat. I forgave him, but he keeps doing it again; I'm not going to be disrespected." To these thoughts and very real emotions, I fully acknowledge that there are circumstances in a marriage that may warrant physical separation. If you are in a physically or emotionally abusive relationship, seek help. You may be a victim of domestic violence if your partner is overly jealous or possessive, exhibits controlling behaviors, is hypersensitive, exhibits explosive behaviors, threatens you, or uses violence. The National Domestic Violence Hotline can help. Visit http://www.thehotline.org/help, or call 1-800-799-7233 or 1-800-787-3224 (TTY) for assistance. They can help you develop a safety plan. God called husbands to love their wives as Christ loved the church; abuse is not a part of this love.

To those whose marital challenges range from adultery to zzzzz (snoring), you will have to answer the same question that I have. Will you love Him?

HIS COMMITMENT TO ME

Faith without works is dead. I've heard this many times, but it wasn't until I answered yes to God's question that I had to live it. In order to love my husband the way God intended, I had to believe in and trust God's commitment to me! This was getting deep. I trust God. I believe God. What does love have to do with it? Everything. God's commitment to me, to you, is this: "For I know the plans I have for you," declares the Lord, "plans to prosper you and not to harm you, plans to give you hope and a future" (Jer. 29:11); "Take delight in the Lord, and he will give you the desires of your heart" (Ps. 37:4); "I can do all this through him who gives me strength" (Phil. 4:13); "I waited patiently for the Lord; he turned to me and heard my cry" (Ps. 40:1); and "Trust in the Lord with all your heart and lean not on your own understanding; in all your ways submit to him, and he will make your paths straight" (Ps. 3:5–6).

God was letting me know that if I believed and trusted in His commitment to me, then I would know that what I was going through is part of a process; I will be shaken but not crushed. It is all for my good; and I will be prosperous, and God will be glorified through my obedience.

So now God wanted to know if I loved Him, enough to believe His commitment to me and to act out that belief. The answer is yes. I may not understand why; it may be uncomfortable, and I may not always like what I'm going through. But because of His commitment to me, I have a money-back guarantee. It is well!

So, the not-so-secret secret is again revealed. The marriage trinity has God at the center. To have a fulfilling and lasting marriage, you have to keep your eye on God and not your spouse. Ask during times of struggle, "God, what do You want me to learn? What are You trying to show me? Will You help me to do Your will?" As you seek to respond to God's active presence and teaching in your life, you will simultaneously give more patience, more grace, and more love to your spouse. Does it sound easy? It's not.

The good news is that while it's not easy, it's also not impossible. It takes active effort. It takes commitment. It takes faith, active faith.

It's a G Thing

Marriage is a G thing, a God thing. Although people and governments have established frameworks, laws, and traditions for marriage by human standards, God created and provided the gift of marriage, the very concept of marriage, to mankind. It's no surprise that so many marriages "don't work." How can something work if you don't follow the user's manual?

Let's say you buy a car, and the user's manual says to use premium gasoline, change the oil every five thousand miles, and rotate the tires every six months. But your friend Shannon tells you that she uses unleaded in her car and has never had a problem. You have fifteen thousand miles on your car and haven't had an oil change, and as it appears to work just fine and the tires aren't bald, you are not worried. What do you think eventually will happen to your car? It may work, but it won't work as long as it was meant to or as well as it was supposed to; you are going to end up putting a lot more money and time into it than you would have if you had followed the user's manual. Eventually, and certainly prematurely, you will sell or dispose of the car, and it will be all the manufacturer's fault. You'll say, "I'll never buy a car made by X again." It becomes easy to repeat these behaviors because we either know someone who didn't follow the instructions and all appears to have worked for them, or because we ourselves didn't follow the instructions at one time and didn't have problems. So we go from car to car and determine good ones from bad ones based not upon our proper utilization of the cars but upon how well the cars did nor did not perform while being mistreated.

Ouch! Let's keep it real. If we are not following the user's manual, we are mistreating our marriages, and we will end up disposing of them prematurely and eventually. The good news is we can avoid this. The user's manual for marriage says, "That is why a man leaves his father and mother and is united to his wife, and they become one flesh" (Gen. 2:24) and "Husbands, love your wives, just as Christ loved the church and gave himself up for her to make her holy, cleansing her by the washing with water through the word, and to present her to himself as a radiant church, without stain or wrinkle or any other blemish, but holy and blameless. In this same way, husbands ought to love their wives as their own bodies. He who loves his wife loves himself" (Eph. 5:25–28).

Finally, it also says, "Wives, in the same way submit yourselves to your own husbands so that, if any of them do not believe the word, they may be won over without words by the behavior of their wives, when they see the purity and reverence of your lives. Your beauty should not come from outward adornment, such as elaborate hairstyles and the wearing of gold jewelry or fine clothes. Rather, it should be that of your inner self, the unfading beauty of a gentle and quiet spirit, which is of great worth in God's sight" (1 Pet. 3:1–4).

Remember, this doesn't mean every day will be sunny or that you won't occasionally feel like you want to strangle your spouse, but it does give you instruction for how you should behave, respond, relate, and act when it happens.

I don't know if you are thinking what I was thinking when all of this was revealed to me. I was thinking, "Why do I have to always be the bigger person, the peacemaker, the one who is willing to say I'm sorry first and to forgive? I don't want to; I'm not going to." I came to understand how far away those feelings were from what God was calling me to be, not only as a wife but also as a Christian. Again, if I am a follower of Christ and I'm called to walk in His way and to die to myself daily, then I've answered the question as to why I had to be the one.

By the standards *we* have set for *ourselves*, some women might feel like they are allowing themselves to be mistreated or disrespected when they respond in this manner. I say trust God's commitment to you. He will show you if you trust Him.

Some might say, "I tried all of that, and nothing has changed." Ask yourself these questions:

- Did you seek God's counsel in selecting your mate?
- Did you seek God's counsel before marrying your mate?
- Do you regularly pray for your spouse? Your marriage?

The answers to these questions establish the foundation for your marriage.

Recognizing Love

One of my most indelible memories is a conversation I had with my mother in my early adulthood. She was sharing with me some of the frustrations in her relationship with my father. Particularly, she shared that he wasn't attentive or affectionate. My response was this: "But he brings you mangos."

My mother loved mangos. She was an in-home childcare provider and all-around entrepreneur, selling everything from Avon to Amway and managing a small cleaning contract for the privately held Laundromat in our apartment building. She was basically stuck in the house watching kids until six in the evening, so she didn't get a chance to go to the store or run any errands for herself until the weekends. My dad was a brick mason and often drove a taxicab when construction work was slow or in the off-season. I vividly remember that during the summer months, he would bring home three or four mangos for us at least once a week. Similarly, when he drove taxicabs late at night, he would stop by a local eatery and pick up a bucket of fried shrimp and bring it home at one or two o'clock in the morning for my mom; they would wake us up to share in the feast. While mangos and shrimp are not flowers and candy, they were my father's expressions of love and caring, attentiveness, and affection.

How often do we miss out on the experience of love because we have predefined it in some way that oftentimes we haven't even communicated to our spouses? It's a setup. If I'm only going to be happy if you show me affection in this way or that way, and if I don't tell you but become more disappointed in you every time you fail to show me affection that way, then what? I know what some of you are thinking: "But he should know me by now. I shouldn't have to tell him; if he loved me, then..." This is a fairy-tale standard that the world has set, and very few people—if anyone—will ever live up to it. The hard fact is this: he doesn't know what you are thinking if you don't tell him; he's not a mind reader. No matter how long he has known you or you have been together, he won't ever guess your needs and wants 100 percent of the time. People change over time; so do their wants and needs. Last but not least, love is about accepting, respecting, and embracing others the way they are, not as a condition of the things you want!

So I ask you: Will you love him? Love him just the way he is? Respect and embrace him, his strengths, his flaws, his hopes, his fears, and his love? Or is your love for him a condition of how he meets your needs, fulfills your desires, meets your standards, follows your ways, and respects your needs? I told you this is hard stuff.

The reality is if you are both using the user's manual for love (by the way, God is love), then you will become each other's strength instead of each other's reminder of all that you are not. Imagine a relationship where you are broken (you brought your baggage to the marriage) and your spouse is broken (he brought his baggage to the marriage, too), and you both set your baggage visibly on a scale only to find that they have even weight. Your baggage is no heavier than his, and his is no heavier than yours. But together they stabilize the scale. In too many marriages, people hide or fail to recognize their baggage, so the scales are tilted. Often, even when baggage is recognized, it's judged in ways like "He's got way more stuff going on than I do" or "His issues are far worse than mine" and vice versa. This is how we justify our anger, our resentment, and our frustration: by establishing a belief that one person's issues make him or her a worse or harder-to-deal-with person than the other. The truth is some issues are more complicated; however, in a marriage, when spouses are judged and condemned for their shortcomings, failures, inadequacies, differences, likes, beliefs, or traditions, the relationship becomes as broken as the two individuals.

Instead, marriage was meant as a commitment between two imperfect people who recognize and acknowledge each other's imperfect selves and say, "I love you anyway." How freeing. Someone loves me even though I'm this or that? Someone loves me even though I'm *not* this or that? Love says, "No matter how you are, I am here to help you become who you want to be—bumpy road and all—for better or for worse." Remember that vow.

Another reality is that the person you date and the person you marry may seem like two different people sometimes. My very good friend and coauthor of this book often says that when you date, you are not meeting the individual but that person's representative! That is so funny. You know we put our best foot forward and only tell the good things about our lives and ourselves when we are dating. We share all of our hopes and aspirations as if we are right on the verge of achieving them all, and we only share information about the challenges in our lives if we think it's going to gain us sympathy points in the romance. Does this sound familiar? So how do we marry the "right" guy when we've only met the representative?

Seek God's counsel in selecting your mate. Seek God's counsel before marrying your mate.

If it's too late for that, because you are already married, pray for your marriage and pray for your husband. Most of all, pray for yourself that God will give you the grace, patience, love, and mercy that is needed to maintain a marriage.

Now, I told you that this stuff is hard, but it's not impossible. I'm not sharing these points with you as ideologies or wishful thinking. I've had to walk the road (and am still walking it) through every emotion and experience I'm sharing with you. My husband is not a traveler; in fact, he is very much a homebody, a trait I found attractive in him early on. I didn't want a man who had to be in the streets all the time and who spent more time with his friends than his family. Who knew that having a homebody for a husband would create tension between my desire to travel, be social, and experience some of the finer luxuries of life? I hadn't thought it out that far. I want a restaurant; he wants fast food. I want a resort amenity; he wants the best-rate hotel. I want high quality; he wants the best bargain—so on and so on. Reconciling these personal styles and tastes was a critical part of my maturity process in my marriage. I had to learn to respect his values and differences and not look at them as him being cheap or uncaring. Similarly, he had to learn to respect my values and differences and not look at them as being booshie or self-centered. We are who we are; it doesn't mean we love each other any more or any less.

I had to realize, understand, and respect the baggage we each brought to the marriage. I had to answer yes to God's question regarding will you love him, and I had to surround myself with friends who encourage me and who are cheerleaders for my marriage. Last but not least, each time I get upset and frustrated or feel lonely, neglected, or mistreated, I pray, and God brings to my recollection all of the things that I have learned and reminds me that I said yes. That's all that really matters.

For the readers who feel that their relationship with God is estranged or nonexistent, I can offer this. If you desire a relationship with God, giving Him dominion over your heart, your home, and your marriage is a great place to start. You can do this today. I guarantee that as you experience His love, you will continue to seek Him in other areas of your life, and before you know it, you won't know how you ever did it without Him.

HIS ACCEPTANCE OF ME

What I now realize is that God has been teaching me through all of these trials that He loves me, He accepts me; He cherishes me; He will protect me; and He will keep me. The desire I have had all my life to be accepted is misdirected. I say "is" because, at times, I still battle with the need to feel accepted, included, and desired, but He reminds me that I already have those things in Him and through Him. When I'm reminded of this, I am comforted, and the anxiety of rejection, the sting of deception, and the stench of regret are minimized. I no longer allow these emotions—which tear away at the very being of who God made me to be—to taunt me for long. I can call into my presence the Spirit of the Lord and be reminded of his grace and that my life is being orchestrated by Him: "And we know that in all things God works for the good of those who love him, who have been called according to his purpose" (Rom. 8:28). That is not just a saying; it is a principle, a belief, and the truth. God, when sought and followed, leads our lives. And through the ups and downs, trials and missteps, He is molding us in His likeness, bringing us closer to Him, and revealing Himself more and more to us.

God's question to me now is, "Do you love Me?" If my answer is yes—and it is—then God has commanded to me that I feed His sheep. He has commanded that I focus on my service to Him and not on my own needs; He has commanded that I live in a more perfect way.

Truly believing all of these things, I find that my commitment to fulfilling God's will for my marriage is strengthened. I spend less time—note that I didn't say "no time"—being angry, spiteful, and self-pitying. I allow myself to feel but not to wallow in my feelings. I consciously seek God's grace, as I know that He will ease my burden and trust that He will heal my heart. And He does, every time—not always instantaneously but gradually and deliberately. He allows me to trust in His presence and accept His love. Funny how the thing I've been searching for, yearning for, and missing all my life has been there all along. I was just looking for it in the wrong places. My only challenge now is accepting it, each and every time; submitting to this knowledge; and not allowing my flesh to lead me. I have a wonderful, loving, and caring husband, and I love him. He's not perfect, and neither am I.

I am blessed because God has sent me a circle of friends, all godly married women. We're not perfect women by any means. None of us has a perfect marriage, but we all love our husbands, love each other, and love the Lord. So we spend our time encouraging each other (not enabling each other; that's not a productive friendship) and praying for each other and for each other's marriages. We all have glass houses, so we don't throw stones. We just have a good time. God, through the Holy Spirit, has become flesh, and He surrounds me in the love of these ladies. I pray the same for you.

SELF-REFLECTION QUESTIONS

What baggage did you bring to your marriage? How does it affect your relationship with your spouse?

_____

_____

_____

_____

_____

_____

Is anger, hurt, or resentment creating a stench in your marriage? If so, are you willing to let go of it and forgive?

_____

_____

_____

_____

_____

_____

How do you respond to your spouse when you are hurt? Do you find it difficult to forgive? Why?

_____

_____

_____

_____

_____

_____

Do you have any regrets in your marriage? What are they? How do you plan to overcome them?

_____

_____

_____

_____

_____

_____

CHAPTER 4

HE'S EVERYTHING I ASKED FOR AND MORE

It's amazing. It's fast. It's a journey. We went and
renewed our passports yesterday, and when I looked
at the picture and the date, I realized how quickly ten
years had passed. I said to my husband, "Wow, next time
we get these renewed, we'll be fifty-five and fifty-seven."
My husband has provided me with a place of safety
to spread my wings. He is my rock. He makes me feel
beautiful even on days I can't see it. And then he drives
me crazy by leaving cupboard doors open and tossing
his toothbrush into the sink from the shower like he's
making a basket. He is everything I asked for and more.

THEME: LOVE, LAYERS, AND LISTENING

BEFORE MARRYING ARIC, I had dated the same man for ten years, my entire twenties. He was almost the perfect guy, at least on paper. Ron was going to med school with the dream of becoming an emergency-room doctor. He had model good looks and was athletic and popular in high school. He immediately caught my attention on the first day of a college English class.

But Ron was a mirage. A mirage is defined as an image of a distant object, illusory. The closer you get to it, the further away it moves. You can never quite reach it. It doesn't really exist. That's how it was between us. There were glimpses of connection, moments of closeness and authenticity, that were powerful, and then they would slip away. It was always almost enough, right on the verge of satiating my need for connection and for something real. Then it would become just like the reflection of water in the distance on a hot, steamy road. You think that you'll be able to catch up to it, but you never can because it doesn't really exist. Or maybe I was the mirage—not fully real, realized, or even close to becoming a self-actualized human being.

It took me ten years to realize that what we had would never become anything more. I was always second to his priorities: friends, school, career, and so on. He would say to me, "After I get into med school, you'll be first. After my first year of med school, you'll be first. After I finish med school, you'll be first." It was an echo that grew louder and louder. I started hearing it in my own mind: "After I'm chief of staff, you'll be first. After I retire, you'll be first. After I die, you'll be first!

I came to the realization that you can't put love in a box and save it for some future date. It will expire. Love is not a tangible product that you hand to someone after you've taken care of all of your other goals in life and say, "OK, here it is. I'm giving you my love now!" Love is a living, fluid organism that happens while life itself is happening. It is life! It must be nurtured consistently to grow, blossom, become beautiful, and thrive.

With Ron, I felt like that delicate fern needing to be watered every day or it would quickly start to shrivel and become limp. You know the kind of plant I'm talking about. You forget to water it for a day or two and become horrified when you think it's too late; it's too dry or too far-gone to come back. You water it, over water it, and then breathe a deep sigh of relief when it starts to perk up and once again show signs of life. And then you do the same thing all over again! I was that plant, and Ron would give me just enough water to come back to life each and every time. Unlike the plant, I had the option to leave. As the emptiness with Ron grew bigger and became more painful than the fleeting moments of connection, I knew something had to change.

I had the opportunity to apply for internships around the country as I completed my doctorate in clinical psychology. I was hungry for a change, a move that would make breaking up with Ron and moving on possibly easier. My journey took me from California to Charlotte, North Carolina. I was excited for a year away to learn, reflect, and then, I thought, go back to California.

I knew I had to take some time to process my life from age twenty to twenty-nine. I thought they were years shaped by my relationship with Ron. However, the epiphany I had later was that my years with Ron were actually shaped by an event much earlier in life. What had I learned in my relationship? Why did I stay so long? What did I want next for myself? What type of man did I want to spend my life with? To understand your present and embrace your future, you must first understand what happened in your past, who you are, where you come from, and what your "blind spots" are that get in the way of achieving wholeness and happiness. Delving in and getting to know yourself can be a daunting prospect, to say the least.

Being in North Carolina provided just the time and space I needed to focus on myself and look at the next chapter in my life. The writer Michael Crichton, famous for *Jurassic Park*, once said that spending time in new places allows people to change the background of their lives and, therefore, see the foreground—themselves—more clearly. The backdrop of North Carolina allowed me to see myself more clearly. Changing the background doesn't always have to include a physical move. We can change our backdrops in so many ways by doing whatever jolts our perspective, shakes up our "perceived" reality, and helps us to see things more clearly. Maybe it's taking up meditation or yoga or returning to prayer.

It's so easy to go along with our heads down and tell ourselves that we're too busy to take the time to look up or step back and take inventory of our lives. If we're honest, it's probably easier and less scary to keep our heads down and not take a look at ourselves. But it's definitely not as interesting or rewarding. A dear friend of mine used to say, "We're all just bozos on the bus of life!" The question is do you want to be a passenger or a driver with a GPS and vision of where you are trying to go while, at the same time, enjoying the journey? Turning on cruise control, or autopilot, can be a nice option once in a while, but be wary of looking up years later to discover that you're way off course and have ended up somewhere that you didn't intend to go! Perhaps you didn't have a plan in the first place, but you know this isn't where you want to be. I would say it's a better option to do our research—get to know ourselves—and consciously choose a course with the flexibility of changing direction along the way.

When I got to North Carolina, I decided to enter into therapy to address *my* issues and to learn how to better drive my bus. Ron may not have been perfect, but I certainly wasn't, either. We all have blinders on. I could partially see the things that were blocking me from becoming the best me possible. But how would I fix them? I grew up in an Irish, Italian (actually Sicilian) family that used the silent treatment, so brushing things under the rug, disconnecting from emotion, and not saying how I feel had been "successfully" passed on to me and had become my own form of communication. I used these techniques beautifully with Ron and other important people in my life. Maybe Ron was the perfect fit at that time in my life. The fact that he only got so close allowed me to keep my distance. A match made in heaven!

Are You Ready to Change?

As I embarked on my own personal journey and began to connect with who I was, I knew I wanted something different in a relationship...but what did that look like, and how would I find it? First comes the acknowledgment that some things aren't working in your life. Maybe they had served a purpose but not anymore. I do believe we attract people based on where we are in our lives. If I wanted to attract someone different, I had to change. I had made it to the first step: realizing that change was needed and that change had to start with me.

I knew I wanted to live more authentically and be present and as real with people as possible. But this was very scary to me. What if they don't like the "real" me, the honest me? How would I handle conflict? Ron and I retreated to distancing when things got dicey; this behavior was comfortable because it's what I had grown up with. My parents could go days around the house just ignoring each other. It was truly an art. My sisters, brother, and I learned the strategy very well. It was amazing how well we all played along!

I started clarifying what I wanted for my life and believing I was worthy of the vision I was crafting through hard work and introspection. I wanted to be with someone who didn't brush things under the rug. I wanted a relationship where what you see is what you get, for better or worse! I wanted someone who was going to be my partner in life, my equal. I wanted to be the most important thing in the world to that person, and I wanted that person to have that same place in my life. I wanted that in the present, not the promise of it at some distant point in a future that may never come. I wanted two well-watered happy ferns living side by side!

What I learned in therapy was that change happens through making small tweaks and practicing new behavior until it feels natural. We don't get messed up overnight, and we certainly don't go from the aha moment to the new us overnight! One of my aha moments was realizing that often times I would have an internal response to something someone said but not respond in the moment. I would shut down and dismiss my hurt or my anger. But the feelings didn't go away; they would be stored up, only to come out later in a delayed and often unhealthy way. This led to a lot of resentment and frustration in my relationships. But once I made this connection, I could work on it. I practiced mustering up the courage, even though it was uncomfortable, to say how I felt in the moment. Or if not right in the moment, sooner than usual until the time between feeling the emotion and verbalizing a response grew closer and closer. I must admit that things didn't always come out in an elegant or refined way in the beginning! I also learned that even if you don't say something right away, you can give yourself permission to bring it up later. I also stopped worrying about protecting other people's feelings more than my own. These realizations changed my life. And now I have to be careful not to go too far in the other direction! It feels good to grow!

Ironically, or not so ironically, after my time in therapy had given me a clear vision for what I wanted and some new tools in my toolbox, Aric entered into my life! I have learned that having a clear vision for anything you want out of life is really a prerequisite for achieving it. One of my very best friends introduced us on Halloween night in 1998. It's funny when I look back. She described me to him as a psychologist from California, and she described him as a former marine from Pennsylvania. I think we both initially reacted in the same way: "This person is way too different than me!" He stereotyped me as an overly touchy-feely type, and I envisioned a very rigid, conventional type. I think my friend saw past the surface and knew us both well enough to know we would connect on a much deeper level, a level that truly mattered. We married in September 2002, and ever since, I've felt certain that I'm his number-one priority and partner in life. He's everything I asked for *and* more.

Do You See the Layers?

There are layers to all of us. That is part of the fun and mystery of getting to know someone. Sometimes we're attracted to the top layer without looking any deeper, and when the other layers are revealed, we're either pleasantly surprised, confused, unbalanced, or, quite frankly, not digging those other layers! Perhaps it was luck or a subconscious glimpse into Aric's deeper layers that attracted me to him. But I like those deeper layers to him—well, most of them, most of the time!

We had a friend over one night, and we were all sitting on the deck and talking over a glass of wine. Aric walked away, and when he was out of earshot, Matt, a close friend of my husband, said, "I love that dude." I responded with, "What do you love about him?" He said, "You know, he may have this sort of gruff exterior, but underneath he has a really big heart. He's a good guy." I told Matt that I was so happy that he saw that in Aric. Some people don't get the privilege of seeing the deeper layers. Aric doesn't let everyone in that far to see his big heart.

It made me think about my own layers—with whom I share them and under what conditions. I guess that's what it really comes down to: When you stack up the person's layers, do you like him or her? Are you only seeing the ones you want to see, or are you being honest and really seeing the whole person? Are there more layers that align with yours or not? Aric's not perfect, but I like his most of his layers and can live with the others! Can you identify some of the layers in your mates? How would you describe them? Generous, loyal, brave, impatient, and caring? Equally important, if not more important, is, how would you describe your own layers? What are they? That may be a harder one to answer. Maybe the question is what do you want your layers to be? By working on ourselves, we inevitably change the dynamic in any relationship.

Embracing another person's layers requires compassion. We are often so hard on ourselves and subsequently hard on others. I know it is hard to do, but sometimes just pausing, refraining from judgment, having compassion for other people's origins, and accepting who they are in this world can take a little pressure off a relationship. We all come into relationships with a past that drives us and blinds us to some degree. Bringing values from each of our own families about money, love, and life and expecting that all of these layers will line up perfectly just isn't realistic! What's amazing is how little most of us talk about these things before taking the plunge into marriage! Do we ask, "Are you a spender or a saver? How ambitious are you? Where do you see yourself in ten years? What are your values? Are birthday cards important to you?" It's funny; perhaps we think we know the answers, but as time goes on, we can be surprised or even blindsided by the answers and the layers that our spouse begins to reveal!

After being together sixteen years, I think I'm starting to really "get" Aric. That's amazing, isn't it? I'm still learning! We had a conversation recently where he told me that living in a big nice house was never really that important to him. I said, "What? I never knew or thought that!" I almost felt deceived. Having a nice big home was a really important value growing up in my own family and one I have to admit I've inherited. Sometimes, we'd go to McDonald's as a family, and my sisters, brother, and I would be allowed to order only two items. But we lived in a four-thousand-square-foot custom-built home with room for horses! It could be quite confusing growing up in our house sometimes. Hearing this from Aric caused me some anxiety. Who are you? I wondered. I thought we were on the same page! He said if we hadn't met, he'd probably be living on a boat somewhere.

I know him and love him as he is, but he, too, is becoming more of who he always was before life interrupted, if that makes sense. And I'm also becoming more of who I am. We're all works in progress. Luckily, most of our values are still compatible at the core! I think that's what life's journey is all about. Who we are is already there, deep inside of each of us, and it's our job to help those people come out, grow, and reach their potential. In some ways, it seems, ironically, we're all working to come full circle.

When I look back at myself when I was six, seven, or eight years old, I see who I am now. We're probably our most authentic selves at that early age. I started my first business as a kid, selling baby mice "pinkies" to the local pet store for twenty-five cents each. I still remember the feeling of excitement that someone had agreed to "do business" with me and wanted what I had to offer! However, you can imagine my horror when I learned later that the baby mice were used to feed the snakes! Yikes.

I was a dreamer and a leader of the other children in my neighborhood. My best friend Deedee and I created "The Animal Club" where we would gather the younger kids, teach them about animals, and give them homework assignments. To our surprise, they would listen to us and show up every week after school! Forty years later, I still have my treasured Animal Book with all of the poems and stories we created on Sparkleberry Street. Yes, this is the actual name of the street I lived on until I was ten years old. And the name is quite fitting.

As a young girl on Sparkleberry Street, I didn't struggle with responding in the moment or connecting with my emotions. It was natural for me to react in an unfiltered manner and just be who I was; I didn't predict how people would respond to my response, how others would feel, or what they would do once I said what I had to say. I was still young and hadn't perfected the dysfunctional coping mechanisms that I would later have to undo before finding myself again later in life. I realize that having some censorship abilities and thinking before you blurt things out are healthy and part of our development. But I took it too far, which worked for me at the time but hindered me as a young adult. When I reflect on those early years on Sparkleberry Street, they felt so unencumbered and free. They were almost magical.

One of those magical experiences was when I was seven years old and received my favorite brown faux-leather coat with sheepskin trim around the collar and cuffs. This was my magic coat. In the pocket, there was a handful of differently colored round pieces of paper. I'm still not sure, but I think they were the leftover pieces that come from a hole puncher. The coat was secondhand, and I found them shortly after my parents gave me the coat. I examined these little round pieces of paper and their different colors: red, blue, orange, and yellow. I pulled my hand out of my pocket, and they felt like a surprise—an extra little gift that came with the coat. They felt magical to me in some way.

I don't know how it started; but one day my older brother Mike was tormenting me, chasing me, and I knew I wasn't getting away this time. Suddenly, I put my hand in my pocket and pulled out one of the little round pieces of paper. I whirled around, faced him, and stopped dead in my tracks. With one of the "magic" orange-colored dots held up in front of me, I said, "You better stop. If I pop this magic dot in my mouth, I'll be stronger than you!" I said it with such belief and such intensity that Mike just stood there looking bewildered and confused about what to do next. He tried to break me down a bit by saying, "You're making that up. That's not magic." But I didn't wane in my belief, again exclaimed how powerful and magical the piece of paper was, and told him he dare not make me put it in my mouth and swallow it. From that day on, whenever I needed protection from my brother, I whipped out the magic dots from my old brown coat with confidence, and it worked every time.

I understand now why he believed me. I could have pulled out a carrot and possibly had the same effect. It was the confidence I exuded and the belief in what I possessed that stopped him in his tracks. I did not display doubt or seem unsure in any way. But somewhere along the way, I stopped believing in the power of those little dots in my coat pocket. Somewhere along the way, they lost their bright color and became thinner and thinner until they eventually began to disintegrate and disappeared. I think that was the beginning of losing the belief in my own power. I stopped trusting my inner strength. I, too, was a brightly colored dot that began to lose her color and began to fade away inside myself.

How do we get to that place of losing our brightness and our power? How do we begin to not believe in ourselves and stop trusting what we have to offer? How do we get to that place of not feeling or trusting our thoughts, our actions, and our whole being? When do we just hand over our power to others and the world at large? When do we give away our own magical dots to someone else? When does our voice become less important than someone else's? It happens so slowly that often we don't even see the changes. We don't see the light in our soul being chipped away, and then one day we're at this place and not quite sure how we really got there. Even scarier is that sometimes we don't even realize it's happened.

I understand now how I got there. This magical time was before I bought into the family silent treatment and silenced my own emotions because it was too hard otherwise. The magical time was before my mom was an alcoholic, before my brother began using drugs and became labeled as a "juvenile delinquent," and before my dad left our family alone to deal with it all on our own. It was before I became a high school dropout, before the silence and disconnection had grown so loud and big in our family that nothing seemed to matter. The magical time was before what I call my "dormant period" when I was still light and bright and believed in the power of believing, the power of myself, and the power of something bigger than all of it: God, the universe, whatever you want to call it.

When I boil it all down, I'm on a journey to become the person I was before my dormant period. My journey is taking me full circle, and, fortunately, Aric is there with me along for this ride. He is one of the bright and shiny magic dots in my life!

THERE'S MORE CHANGE?

You don't just come full circle, work out all the kinks in the layers, and put your feet up! You just don't arrive and are done now! For better or worse, the process is never truly done. Change is the only constant. Things change. Life changes, and it's sometimes within your control and sometimes not. Of course, positive change, such as a raise in salary, a bigger house, or a new car, is always easier. But what happens when change challenges your comfort zone? When your husband decides to start a new business financed by your 401(k) or wants to take on a home renovation to save money? You know what I'm talking about!

On our first date, Aric told me he told me he wanted to get out of the corporate world and start his own business. He was tired of the politics and living someone else's dream. He wanted to apply his engineering talents and pursue his passion of fixing and fabricating things; he wanted to use both his brain and his hands. I was 100 percent supportive on that first date! What did I care? I didn't know if we would ever see each other again! I said, "Wow, that sounds great. I think you should go for it!" And so he did!

When we met, he drove a luxury car with nice leather interior and wore a suit and an expensive watch. Shortly after we moved in together, he went for it and actually did start his own business; he traded in the car for a pickup truck and the suits for overalls embossed with "Aric" and dropped a zero off his paycheck! He handed me his Tag Heuer watch and said, "Let's take a couple of links out of it. It's your turn to do the corporate thing." Yikes. I panicked. Sure, I supported his dreams, but this was a bit much. What did I expect? I said I wanted a guy who was present, authentic, and honest. He followed through with exactly what he said he was going to do!

You can't just embrace the values and the layers of someone when it's convenient. Remember the vow of "in good times and bad"? Maybe we shouldn't even look at it in terms of good and bad. It's really about balance. Life is all about balance, and marriage is all about integrating two lives into one balanced whole that works.

Just as we have to find balance within ourselves, we have to find balance in the relationships outside of ourselves. Think about that for a second. What does it mean to find balance in relationships outside of ourselves? You can't just take the parts you want and dismiss the rest. You don't order up a man, select only the qualities and traits that you want, and say, "No thanks, I don't need those other parts." You get the whole package! So you must pick carefully. In order to do that, you must know what you want and what you need. Aristotle said, "The energy of the mind is the essence of life. Knowing yourself is the beginning of all wisdom."

If knowing yourself is the beginning of all wisdom, knowing yourself is truly the answer to finding happiness and balance in life and in relationships. The hard part is that sometimes we enter into relationships, into marriage, without truly knowing ourselves. What happens when we begin to know ourselves, become wiser, and start to question our choices, our happiness, and our marriage? How do we continue when our eyes are wide open and we start seeing parts of the package that we didn't see before? Parts of the package that we perhaps wouldn't have chosen if we had the wisdom we have now? Scary stuff, I know.

WHAT'S YOUR SHARED VISION?

What if you still love each other but start wanting different things because relationships aren't static? Sometimes the timing is just off, and you are at different places at different times. Aric and I have very different time lines. Because I went to grad school, his career life began much earlier than mine. When I was ready to start my own business, he had already been running his for a decade and was starting to itch for something different. He dropped out of the corporate world because he didn't want to play the game and wanted to pursue his own dreams.

Remember earlier when I shared my surprise when Aric told me that living in a home was never a big goal or value of his? Well, I should have known one day that those values and his free-spirited qualities would mean him wanting to pursue his other dream of living a nontraditional lifestyle aboard a boat and exploring the world. Well, as I said before, change is constant. Recently, he has become more and more focused on making this new lifestyle a reality, which has started causing me panic, anxiety, and feelings of pressure.

Living aboard a boat and exploring the world sounds amazing, and I definitely foresee a chapter in my life when we just let go and embark on this adventure. But when is the timing right? Our initial conversations felt very all-or-nothing, which was very scary and elicited lots of questions. What about my "stuff"? What if I hate it? What if I'm not ready to say *bon voyage* to the comforts of a home on land? Does that make me a bad person? What if I'm in the middle of my dream of growing my business? Do I just shut the door and walk away from all that I have invested?

It was becoming a bit overwhelming to think about making this huge choice.

How do you both grow without suffocating the other person's passion? I didn't want to deny Aric his dreams or me my own. I was struggling with how to navigate these waters—no pun intended. Now you're starting to understand that he is what I asked for *and* more.

I think if you're in your marriage for the long haul, the answer to growing, changing, and not suffocating or giving up your own dreams and dying within yourself is all about compromise from both individuals. There is always a way through if you want to get through.

ARE YOU LISTENING?

Getting through begins with listening. You must listen to God or the "universe," however it is you define that higher voice that is there for you. It will tell you if you're on the right track; it will nudge you and provide light and guidance for your path. The right people and answers will reveal themselves when you need them and when you're listening.

I was on an airplane and was just reflecting, being quiet, and making some notes about the pros and cons of giving up "everything" and going cruising with Aric. I was feeling anxious inside about this all-or-nothing proposition when a gentleman with an interesting accent sitting next to me suddenly said, "You seem like a very thoughtful person." I thought, How does he know if I'm a thoughtful person or not? Maybe he could see one of my deeper layers? Or maybe he was just hitting on me! I told him I was just sort of doodling about the prospect of going sailing versus continuing on the path I was already on with my business. He looked at me and said, "Why can't you do both?"

He stopped me in my tracks. Why hadn't I thought of that? Does life have to be so black and white? I'm always telling people how wonderful it is that we live in a time where you can work from anywhere and how it's possible to create a career that works for your life versus the other way around. I was so close to the situation that I couldn't see the possibilities!

Here was this stranger who could clearly see there were options rather than one right or wrong path. I just sat there, overwhelmed with excitement at the thought of creating a lifestyle where we would have a little bit of both. All of a sudden, my mind was reeling with possibilities! What if we could just enjoy sailing the Chesapeake Bay, which is right in our backyard, on weekends? Then maybe we could spend a couple winter months in the Florida Keys, and, who knows, maybe we could rent out our house and live on the boat in the Bahamas for a year and work remotely! All of a sudden, I was completely energized by the possibilities. I started making notes about the steps to get there and could visualize it becoming a reality. I will be forever grateful for this person who seemed to appear at just the right time. Was it just luck or coincidence that he was in 10B? I tend to think not. In that moment, this question came to me: Are you doing life, or is life doing you? I choose the former.

Does That Dream Come with a Plan?

So here we are. My vision, my dream—*our dream*—is that we spend part of our time living on the boat and part of our time on dry land. How amazing will that be, and why can't we create it? Your dreams will never come true if you don't know what they are or don't believe they can actually happen. It starts with believing in and owning the belief on a truly visceral level and seeing it as a reality.

About six months after I met the guy in 10B, we did it! We bought the boat. Her name is Exodus. What a perfect name for our exit plan. We decided, if not now, when? Let's start to make our dream a reality.

It's kind of crazy how we got here and how we'll navigate the next phase. But I'm proud of how we did it. We both had our own criteria for what we needed and wanted in a boat and a lifestyle, and we are finding a way to move toward that with compromise while staying true to ourselves.

I don't know exactly when we'll set sail for an extended trip or if we'll ever live full time on the boat. But it doesn't really matter. Life is a journey, and we're embracing it together. We're planning, dreaming together, and sharing our feelings—the excitement and anxiety—all of it in an honest way. Believe me, we're far from perfect; our layers sometimes rub each other the wrong way, and we have to work through it! But we're excited for the future, and we're happy today. My dormant period is over. I have lots of magical dots in my pocket. They are my husband, my circle of women friends with whom I've coauthored this book, many other special people in my life, and life itself. I've found that girl on Sparkleberry Street again and so much more. I can't wait to see what happens next! I encourage you to be brave, take a look inside, change your backdrop once in a while, and listen. You will be heard.

Self-Reflection Questions

In the story, the author talks about different colored magical dots. What do the magical dots represent? Who or what are the magical dots in your life, and are they faded and tattered or bright and whole?

_____

_____

_____

_____

_____

_____

The author talks about blind spots that get may get in the way of achieving wholeness and happiness. Can you identify your blind spots?

_____

_____

_____

_____

_____

_____

The author talks about the choice we have to be drivers or passengers on the bus of life. Which are you? Explain.

_____

_____

_____

_____

_____

_____

CHAPTER 5

THROUGH IT ALL

As a little girl, I had it all planned out. I couldn't wait to get married and start a family of my own. Mr. Right would find me and sweep me off of my feet. We would get married, have four children, and live happily ever after. We met and married, and I thanked God for sending me a good man. But because he hadn't received the same teaching that I had about marriage, we began to clash on some things. I realize now that as we continue to grow, we continue to learn.

THEME: PERSEVERANCE AND FAITH

I TAKE YOU to be my lawfully wedded husband, to have and to hold from this day forward, for better or for worse, for richer, for poorer, in sickness and in health, to love and to cherish, from this day forward until death do us part. Really? So if things don't work out, does that mean it's OK to kill him? Just kidding!

I often find myself repeating and trying to decipher the true meaning of the traditional wedding vows. In his article "Why Do We Make Marriage Vows," Pastor Steve Highlander writes, "Marriage traditions and customs differ greatly from culture to culture, but nearly every culture has them. Through the ages, men and women of all races and religions have chosen to single out a time and place to 'unite in marriage.' Customs guide it; laws govern it; society respects it." Genesis states, "Therefore shall a man leave his father and mother, and shall cleave unto his wife: and they shall be one flesh" (Gen. 2:24). Now that is a challenge, but it can be done! Can you mentally imagine two people becoming one? I've come to the conclusion that this has to be the reason why marriage is difficult at times: two people coming together, living together, and getting to know each other intimately, physically, and emotionally—not necessarily in that order.

As a little girl, I had it all planned out. I couldn't wait to get married and start a family of my own. My Mr. Right would find me and sweep me off of my feet. We would get married, have four children, and live happily ever after. I would love him with everything that I had, and he would love me the same, if not more. We would never go to bed angry with each other. Any problem that we would have, we would take to the Lord in prayer, and once we prayed about it, God would help us to work it out. Divorce would not be an option. Ephesians states, "So ought men to love their wives as their own bodies. He that loveth his wife loveth himself" (Eph. 5:28). My plans had us so much in love that we could face anything or anybody together. We would love each other forever!

I guess you are wondering where these ideas came from. Allow me to tell you a little about my childhood. While growing up, I remember having five generations in our small town. My great-grandmother passed when I was seventeen years old and a senior in high school. Family has always been important to me. Having a father, a mother, and several children living under the same roof was my fantasy; even though that wasn't the case for me growing up, I knew that one day when I got married, it would come true. I would work really hard to keep my marriage and my family together. Growing up, family wasn't the only very important thing to me; family values were, too. The men would look out for the women, and we would stick together. When you messed with one... Well, you know how that goes.

My mother's father, my grandfather whom I very fondly called Poppa, was a Church of God in Christ preacher and a very strong male figure in my life and in our community. I remember him teaching and preaching the word of God. He taught me to study the Word for myself so that I would not be fooled by any false doctrine.

As I grew up under my grandfather's reign, he instilled in us to love the Lord with all of our hearts. We were taught at a young age to trust in God for all things. Poppa would have us read and study the Bible. He would ask us questions and give us money when we answered the questions correctly. He taught us that God was all knowing and that if we turned our life over to Him (got saved), our souls would go live in heaven for eternity when our earthly bodies died. I was raised reading the King James Version of the Bible, and anyone who knows me knows that I favor that version even now. I remember that back then no matter what I was going through, I could find comfort in the scriptures. I remember thinking that there was a scripture for everything. I remember my first experience reading the chapters in the book of Song of Solomon: oh my, poetry at its finest!

We were taught to trust God to send us our spouse; we were taught that dating should lead to marriage and that when doing so, we should not be "unequally yoked." First Corinthians states, "Be ye not unequally yoked together with unbelievers: for what fellowship hath righteousness with unrighteousness? and what communion hath light with darkness" (2 Cor. 6:14). At the time, I didn't quite get the meaning of this verse, but as time went on and I got married, I got a clearer understanding, at least I think I did. While my grandfather was teaching us the Word and having us study the Word, my grandmother taught us how to be ladies and how to prepare ourselves for marriage. We were taught a few simple things, like the way to a man's heart was his stomach. I prided myself in learning how to cook at an early age, and I used to love being in the kitchen with my mom, big sister, aunties, and grandmothers. My mom was the best cook ever. I learned so much from her just by watching; no one seemed to write down recipes, and if I only knew then what I know now, I would have written everything down. We were taught to not treat anyone better than we treated our own family. If we serve our family on paper plates, we should serve our guest on paper plates. We were also taught to let our man know how important he is, to appreciate him, and, most importantly, to keep him satisfied and not to turn him down when he wants...you know.

While the girls were being groomed to be good wives, the men were taught how to be the breadwinner and the head of the household. They were taught to treat their wives with respect and to love them like they love themselves. The men were also taught that when their wives prepared their meals, they should be ready to eat while the food was hot and to thank their wives for the meal. If the food wasn't good, they should be nice about letting their wives know. They were taught to compliment their wives, make them feel appreciated, and let their wives know how important they are. Awarding their wives with gifts to show their appreciation would pay off as well. (I won't dwell on that because I think you get the picture.) This is how I expected my marriage to be.

I remember talking to my mom about marriage and her telling me that when you are deciding if the man that you are with is the right one, check out how he treats and loves his mother because that is probably how he will love and treat you. Because I didn't grow up with both parents in the same household, I really didn't know what to expect when I finally got married. All I knew was that I wanted my one marriage to last my lifetime. I only had a few serious relationships while I was growing up. My goal in dating was to prepare for marriage. If I was with a man and couldn't see myself with him for the rest of my life, then I wouldn't waste my time dating him because my ultimate goal was to marry. The guys whom I dated had all been gentlemen. Most of them were brought up with the same principles as me, so we knew what to expect from each other. They carried my books while we were in school, held my hand while strolling through the malls, opened my car doors, pulled my chairs out for me, walked on the outside, and showered me with gifts. These are the things that I thought my husband would do for me.

A lot of the church girls my age got married after graduation; some went to college and then got married. I went to college as well, moved back home for a while, and then joined the military. Once I finished basic training and technical training school, I was sent to my permanent duty station. The first day at my first duty station I met the guy whom I would marry. We met and married within six months, and I thanked God for sending me a good man. We spent a few months stateside, and then we changed duty locations and went overseas. For the next few years, we got to really know each other, and life was good. When we had problems, we had to work them out without any family interference because to pick up the phone to call to the States was very expensive. I learned to trust him more and lean on him. He was my rock! He wasn't raised the way I was raised, but he was raised well. He was the head of the house, a good provider, and a good friend. I only wished that he would go to church with me. I'm still praying about that to this day. Because he hadn't received the same teaching that I had received about marriage, we began to clash on some things. I realize now that as we continue to grow, we continue to learn.

What happened to the marriage and family that I had fantasized about? There was a time in my marriage when I felt that I had lost myself. I was no longer me. I was my husband's wife and my children's mother. By concentrating so much on them, which is what a good wife and mother should do, I somehow lost myself, and instead of my husband and me pulling closer together, I felt like we were drifting apart, sometimes just going through the motions. I always hoped that my husband would be true to me and that if he ever wasn't, he would definitely not let me find out about it. I always hoped that if he no longer wanted to be with me, he would let me know, and we would go our separate ways as friends. I learned that when you have children, they take up a great part of your life, and if you don't balance it right with your children and your spouse, what are you going to do when the children are all grown and leave the house?

Notice that when I first started talking about one marriage forever, I wasn't married. Now that I have been married for almost thirty-five years, I understand why some people don't stay married. I also understand, believe it or not, why some spouses want to kill each other. Communication plays a very important part in every relation; when you don't communicate, things can get pretty bad. If you find yourself falling into this trap, stop! Get it together, and trust God to open up the communication in your marriage and to be the center of it.

Some of my friends have gone through things within their relationships that have caused them to not make it. I never knew that my marriage and my faith would be tested to the degrees they have been. I was taught how to get a husband and how to keep a husband, but I was not taught about how to stay when the going got tough. I thought that we would be in love forever. You know, love conquers all. *Not!* I truly can understand what Tina Turner was talking about when she sang in her hit record, "What's love got to do with it? What's love but a secondhand emotion?" Through everything that I have been through—God knows that it has been a struggle—I constantly ask myself what happened and how did I get here? Where did I go wrong, and why did I have to go through certain things in my marriage? Why I should stay? How can I stay and continue to be the woman whom God has called me to be when I sometimes feel like I am so alone? Some of my friends and coworkers talk about being lonely because they are single. I want to tell them so badly that while single people accept that they will sometimes be lonely and married people think they should never feel lonely because they have lifetime partners, marriage doesn't always work that way. What happens when your lifetime partner is no longer your best friend, no longer your rock? What do you do? Do you stay, or do you go?

What did I do? I went back to my roots. I went back to how I was taught. I had to continue to trust God to work it out. He can, and He will. I had to remember that times have changed. Most women can't afford to stay at home to take care of the family. They are working just as much as their husbands, and some of us are making more than our husbands; but he is still the man, and we should make him feel like he is the man. With that said, some adjustments must be made. The man is still the head of the house (whether he acts like it or not). We have to allow him to be the head and put our trust in God to lead our husbands. I had to realize that I don't want my husband to try to change me, so it's not my job to try to change him. I've decided to let God handle him; after all, He made him! I will continue to be the helpmate to my husband that God has called me to be. If I ever go to that dark place again, I will pray my way out; the beauty of talking to God is knowing that He won't tell anybody else. He knows what I'm going through; He knows my heart, and I can trust and depend on Him always. I'm reminded of the words to the song "Through It All," by the late Andraé Crouch:

I've had many tears and sorrows. I've had questions for tomorrow. There's been times I didn't know right from wrong, but in every situation, God gave me blessed consultation that my trials come to only make me strong. I've been a lot of places. I've seen a lot of faces. There's been times I felt so all alone, but in my lonely hours, yes, those precious lonely hours, Jesus let me know that I was His own. I thank God for the mountains, and I thank Him for the valleys. I thank Him for the storms He brought me through. For if I'd never had a problem, I wouldn't know that God could solve them. I'd never know what faith in God could do. Through it all, through it all, I've learned to trust in Jesus. I've learned to trust in God. Through it all, through it all, I've learned to depend upon His Word.

Self-Reflection Questions

Do you and your spouse still have things in common, just the two of you?

_____

_____

_____

_____

_____

_____

Can you still spend the entire day with your spouse and enjoy each other's company?

_____

_____

_____

_____

_____

_____

CHAPTER 6

JOURNEYING TOWARD YOUR PURPOSE, NOT JOCKEYING FOR POSITION

When a girlfriend calls to seek your advice but prefers counsel from the titled husband, feelings of jealousy and ungodly envy can enter in, and it must be decided if you are going to compete or come together, jockey for top billing in the ministry or be one in agreement.

THEME: PRIDE AND ENVY

IT SAYS IN Amos, "Can two walk together unless they have agreed to do so" (Amos 3:3). Who are the two, and what do they have to agree upon? The two is not the husband and wife but the husband and wife plus God. I know you are probably saying to yourself, "That's three." Genesis states that the reason a man leaves his mother and father is because he is united to his wife and they become *one flesh* (Gen. 2:24). This is repeated several times throughout the Bible, so doing the God kind of math, the husband and wife become one in the sight of the One, thereby making two. It's one thing to state this scripture with boldness; it is another thing to live it. Hopefully, you will be encouraged and strengthened to agree to the walk and continue in it with joy.

THE CONFLICT, THE COMMITMENT, AND THE COMPROMISE...IF WE MUST.

Conflict. Wedding vows, unless you chose to write them yourselves, begin with conflict. Now before you try to remember them, let me help you out. We promise that we will love, honor, and cherish during all the following times: for better or for worse (no one goes into the happily ever after believing that it would be anything less), for richer or for poorer (does anyone really "hook up" with his or her significant other, especially during those lean and early days, believing that he or she will have less in terms of riches and wealth?), and—let us not forget the last—in sickness and in health. While some people might go into the marriage knowing that the other person has a fatal or debilitating condition, I am willing to bet that most people go into a marriage believing that the only sickness that they would have to ever endure is when they both get too old for it to matter. Having two very individualized individuals come into a contractual agreement, or covenant, before one God and declare "until death" can be challenging, in the least, after the euphoria of being newlywed diminishes.

Jobs, money, children, social clubs, and, in the case of my husband and me, ministry can all cause conflict within a marriage. Your job may have you travel a lot, work late hours, or have zero-dark-thirty mornings, and those wonderful sunshiny, bring-me-my-coffee-in-bed mornings may become few and far between.

Money, cheddar, change, or that mean green—whatever you choose to call it, can cause major conflict in a marriage. The poorer isn't a factor until it becomes a factor. There is nothing wrong with money; money is fine. What gets us in trouble is the love, longing, and lust for more money. As it is stated in First Timothy, "For the love of money is a root of all kinds of evil, for which some have strayed from the faith in their greediness, and pierced themselves through many sorrows" (1 Tim. 6:10). Most of us don't want to experience the "poorer "part of our vows, so we do all that we can to avoid that part of what we have promised to do. (I can almost imagine these thought bubbles over the bride and groom during that part: "Oh, we will have our love to get us through." That's their first mistake.)

When our love for each other is replaced by the love of the almighty dollar, relationships start to change; they are rearranged for the sake of the dollar in order to provide for the family to avoid eviction and repossession of our possessions. Don't get me wrong; I know that nowadays we all have to do what we need to do to provide for our families. However, I'm talking about the desire to work to get rich. Ask yourself this question: Would you rather your family be wealthy or healthy? Proverbs states that we should not overwork to be rich (Prov. 23:4). Sometimes, it causes one or more members of the happy couple to get anywhere between two to three jobs and, thus, creates more separation and distance.

When distance starts to occur within what is supposed to be happily ever after, it becomes a very real third person in your marriage. Before you know it, what used to be long meaningful talks become short, loud, and curt outbursts and matter-of-fact conversations that are void of any real intimacy and full of the wrong kind of emotion. The "better" that we once believed would be ours for the taking each and every day becomes the "worse." It seems like it happens overnight, but it actually takes time to develop.

Think about it. We go to jobs and have relationships with our co-workers that should be reserved for the spouse whom we have promised to have and to hold from this day forward. We demonstrate courtesy, patience, listening, and laughter toward persons who would otherwise be total strangers if we did not have our jobs in common. We don't make lifelong commitments to these people, yet, more often than not, we choose to compromise with them in more ways than we do in our own marriages.

Compromise is a jewel of a word. It is so very valuable, precious, and necessary for the success of any relationship, and it is the water to the fire that is conflict. Giving up the right to be right, the desire to have the last word, and the need to have it your way can make your marriage—if nothing else—enjoyable, at least until the next conflict arises.

Who does the compromising? The answer is "both." No one person in the relationship should have to compromise more than the other. (Who is keeping track anyway?) We are to "let nothing be done through strife or vainglory; but in lowliness of mind let each esteem other better than themselves" (Phil. 2:3). Following these biblical principles can ensure that compromise is evident and that conflicts are resolved in a timely manner. Being the half of a fractured whole takes work; it takes commitment.

Commitment to the relationship goes well beyond just saying that you are going to remain sexually and intimately committed. This commitment involves overlooking your own desires, wants, and, sometimes, needs; this commitment involves foregoing the girls night out because your marriage or your mate is in need of some tender loving care, a dinner for two, a date night without the kids, and conversation that does not involve diapers, bottles, schools, or homework. I stated earlier that we develop committed relationships with our coworkers. We commit to the office parties, the late nights, and the impromptu meetings. We may complain, yet we still do what is required of us. Why? Because we get something out of it: we get the paychecks, the bonuses, and the benefits. If we apply that same level of commitment to our marriage along with the expectation of getting a payday, a bonus, and, my favorite, the benefits (even if we don't receive the rewards immediately), we will not be disappointed.

SUBMITTING, SOJOURNING, AND SHUTTING UP

Being married to a minister may seem to be a bed of roses compared to other marriage dynamics, right? Wrong! Being married to a minister means that you are married to a man. Whether you have been married for a while, have just got married, or are thinking about marriage, please understand that marriage requires more than prayer. I believe prayer is the most vital of marital ingredients, along with patience, listening, and love; however, prayer isn't the *only* thing you are required to or should do. It means submitting (yes, I said the *s* word), sojourning (staying, dwelling, and abiding together), and *shutting up*. Through prayer, the timing of all of these will be on point and on time. The Bible does tell us that there is a time to keep silent (Eccles. 3:7–8) and, of course, to speak. Personally speaking, I haven't yet fully grasped, or matured into, that pattern; however, I'm grateful that the Lord is both faithful and patient as I continue learning that this is necessary for the health of my marriage and for the sanity of both my husband and me.

Being joined in holy, and sometimes happy, matrimony with a minister of the Gospel of Peace should, in fact, bring peace. Shouldn't it? To some extent, it does—at least until he begins "girlfriend" chatter with your girlfriend or is the only one everyone notices when you are by his side. It means fully understanding that marriage is a ministry—a ministry that is fully evident both in and out of church. When you are at home, when you are at work, and when you are in solitude or around your many friends, *it is a ministry*. The two people in the marriage are held to a God kind of accountability that requires them to minister to the needs of others but mostly to minister to each individual's needs within their God-ordained union. When the internal ministry starts to lack, it has the potential to weaken and not be able to withstand the storms that life will most certainly bring. Here is one of my needs. I find that not being recognized with my husband is an issue for me. Do I know that this will not always happen? Yes. Does this make it easier when situations arise where I am not acknowledged as his wife? *No!*

I believe God has a solution to my problem of feeling second best, second rate, and second fiddle in the eyes of, as I sometimes believe, everyone—including family and most of our friends, female and male alike. I sometimes want to give in to that feeling and stand up in the middle of an empty, and sometimes not-so-empty, room and scream, "Hey, I am here, too!" I know, all too well, that I am an original, designed and desired by God to be in fellowship with Him, to be in relationship with Him, and, of course, to be a part of His discipleship and of any other "ship" pertaining to the personal and private association that comes with service unto Christ. However, underneath the spirituality, holiness, and righteousness that I desire and seek to acquire, there are brokenness and hurt, rejection and dejection, and some pain and sadness.

When I think about being placed on the back burner while my husband is the pot that is being watched, one incident comes to mind. One particular afternoon we played hooky from work, not to do anything special but just to rest. This rest was needed to be about God's business with freshness. During this day of rest, I received a phone call from a really good girlfriend whom we will call Terry. She was going through a marital issue, as we all do from time to time.

Terry is one of those girlfriends whom I had in my Before Christ (BC) days. When we were in different parts of the world, we each developed a relationship with Him, walked with Him, and proclaimed Him to others. We were not in contact with each other during this part of our development, shaping, and molding. God was doing a mighty thing in both of us, at the same time and at the same pace.

My dearest friend Terry is also a minister, but she is also a woman and a daughter of God first. She had landed in a pickle of a situation: almost losing her own unsaved husband to adultery, among other things. We understand that evil spirits don't usually come alone. Matthew states that:

> When an evil spirit comes out of a man, it goes through arid places seeking rest and does not find it. Then it says, "I will return to the house I left." When it arrives, it finds the house unoccupied, swept clean and put in order. Then it goes and takes with it seven other spirits more wicked than itself, and they go in and live there. And the final condition of that man is worse than the first. That is how it will be with this wicked generation. (Matt. 12:43–5)

Terry started talking to me about her situation and overheard my husband in the background. She stated that she really needed to speak to him. I thought, Really?

Now don't get me wrong. I am not jealous. I have never been jealous, and as a twenty-five-plus-year-old woman, I was not about to begin that foolishness now. I put the call on speaker, and she proceeded to tell my husband Chris that she needed to speak to another preacher (not minister). So I handed the phone to him, and he began to give her worldly, unsound, flesh-driven advice. When I stepped in and spoke up, she dismissed my correction, and he was then fueled by her affirmation. I backed down immediately. But I felt angry and a little hurt, and a whole lot of arrogance began to rise in me. I prayed under my breath and bit my lip.

The conversation continued, and then the Holy Spirit began to take control. My dear husband began to speak what thus sayeth the Lord (prayer works). All of sudden, she *heard* him. This is the conversation that went on in my head: "Chick, really. I've been telling you to gird your loins and your heart. I've been telling you to pray earnestly and boldly, around your husband and in private. I repeated to you, over and over again, that you can do all things through Christ who strengthens you. So now, because my preacher husband is here and has said these very same things that I said to you in *our* private conversations, you consider him, my dear husband, a relationship expert. *Really?*"

That spirit of jealousy had quickly risen up, and it consumed my being for the rest of the day. It destroyed my peace and eradicated my rest. The Lord ministered unto me that my mind should be always clothed with the armor of light (Rom. 13:12) and that my focus should be on mimicking the character of Jesus and not on giving into foolish and wicked jealousies. Jealousy had made an entrance and brought along with it its friends anger and quarrelsomeness. Jealousy rarely makes an appearance by itself. (I will cover the reasons for this later on.) This was certainly not a good time for me to bring any word to anyone but the Lord. I couldn't talk to my husband; he would've counted it as childishness. I am not advocating the suffering-in-silence mentality, but I knew in my spirit that I needed to consult my Father, my Maker. I knew that this was one of those shut-up moments. I had to ask myself the question "Why did I allow that situation to take me to jealousy?"

My answer came quickly. I just wanted to be heard; I wanted to be acknowledged, and I wanted to be affirmed. I wanted to be the drum major. Terry wasn't the only one being ministered to that day. God had to show me that I was just as vital, just as important to the kingdom and to my husband's ministry, as my husband was. I had to understand that the only person really placing importance on titles was me! Terry and Chris weren't doing it. I had to realize that we are in the business of kingdom building, demonstrating a ministry of marriage together as one, and journeying, sojourning, and walking together. In agreeing with God that we are the two who are walking together, my husband and I are one, and God is one who together with us equals two.

This seems like an easy-enough lesson that should have taken me into the rest of my life. A lesson like that sticks to you and in you like good oatmeal, right? Three years later, our careers moved us from one destination to another. We left one church and had to seek, search, and find another place of worship, establish relationships, and develop connections with other believers.

Chris and I found the church, the house of God, that suited our family's needs and that, most importantly, showed the love of God that we were in desperate need of. During this time, my husband was in school, as was I, and during this time, I was doing two sets of homework: mine and reviewing and correcting his. Because I attempt to be the dutiful spouse, try to be the really helpful helpmate, and am committed to the cause, I was inundated with the stuff of life instead of living it. While my husband was growing in the grace and knowledge of Christ, I was growing in the knowledge of his work and my work. This is the journeying.

During this time, this journey, this trek, this conflict, we have both had opportunities to minister to the people of God, and both of us have confessed to feeling the tinge of jealousy when it comes to those ministry opportunities.

Jealousy is a funny yet not-so-funny thing; when you have tasted it once, you will not ever forget that taste. This is a perplexing thing: that such a small emotion, thought, idea, or inkling can affect not only your attitudes but those of your entire household. But wasn't God a jealous God? How come I can't be jealous? How come I can't stomp my foot, poke my lip out, and sulk over opportunities that were never mine? How come?

The reason for this is because I was not experiencing jealousy but *envy*, the sinful and "soulish" sensation that destroys the strongest of relationships. God has a right to be jealous because we belong to Him; we were created in Him and for Him. Jealousy, godly jealousy, is more of a protective posture that God has with us rather than an envious one. Envy projects that we desire something that we never had, that we want what was never offered to us, and that we yearn for something we were never meant to have.

I have been in situations where I was flat-out envious of an opportunity that never had my name on it, was never was offered to me, and was never meant for me to have.

Where could I place blame for this envy? Should my husband have suggested to those who invited him that I play a part because I'm powerful in my prayers and move the people to tears?

Should those who invited my husband "pick up" on my anointing, appoint me to a position next to my dear husband, and allow us to minister in sync? Shouldn't I have been chosen, elected, and selected to minister with my family? Shouldn't I? Shouldn't we? Shouldn't he?

Well, one thing is for sure: I would never want to take the place of God, and I was promptly reminded that my prayers are answered by the selection of being nonselected. When God selected and elected me to be hidden in His shadow and in His safety, I realized that it was not a slight but was the solution to my neediness in this area. One of the prayers that I offer up to the Lord is "Lord, prepare me greatly for your people" and "Allow me to not bring you to shame." God is a prayer-answering God. I just could not see it at the time.

I found it shameful and embarrassing that I experienced such an emotion for someone whom God has given unto me and has dutifully placed as the man of the house; however, I asked for clarity on this and had to overcome it because according to Revelation, "the accuser of the brethren has been cast down and that I am overcome by the blood of the Lamb and the word of My testimony" (Rev. 12:10–1). What this has done for me personally is to allow me to identify that if such an emotion can be stirred up in me, the helper of my husband's needs and vision, then it could be stirred up in those who watch from the outside and who do not fully understand the complexities on the inside. This has allowed my own battle with fleshly emotions to make me better and more mature in the things of God for the people of God. Enduring this inner conflict has encouraged me to tell my emotions, "Sit down somewhere, and shut up!"

Envy is not the only way to destroy a marriage. Usurping is another. I can really identify with how Eve was misled in the garden into going after that fruit that was good, pleasing, and desirable (Gen. 3:6) because in marriage when "the lust of the eyes, the lust of the flesh, and the pride of life" (1 John 2:16) take hold and rise up, it's very difficult (notice I did not say "impossible") to combat and control. Usurping the authority that has been put in place is a by-product of pride. When we seek to overlook or overtake the leader (as Satan did with God), the root of that is pride. We start to believe the lie that the leader is incapable, incompetent, and, sometimes, insane. We think along the terms that "we can do and be better" at the task at hand than the leader.

Another consequence of pride is jealousy. I stated earlier that I wanted to be the drum major. Dr. Martin Luther King, Jr.'s sermon "The Drum Major Instinct" states that he if were to be called a drum major, then let him be called a drum major for peace and a drum major for righteousness. Yours truly was attempting to be a drum major for acknowledgment and attagirls, all because of pride. Pride is envy's best friend in the whole world, its BFF (best friend for life). It accompanies envy at every juncture and junction. Having to fight to be heard or seen is prideful, especially if you desire for your harassing, your nagging, or your badgering to be heard rather than your helpfulness. (I know that you are probably thinking, "I'm not harassing, and I am being helpful." Yes, you are being helpful...to you.) That is pridefulness. One way to combat this evil is to ask yourself if you would listen to you if you spoke in that tone of voice and had that facial expression. If the answer is no or if you took too long to answer, it's pridefulness.

Pride will have you accepting invitations to events and committing to outings without consulting your husband and then expecting him to go along with them, without complaining and with excitement. Pride will have you believing that your time is more valuable than your family's and that if it's good for you, then it's good, period. Pride coupled with its BFF envy can have you acting impulsively on a thing that could potentially harm you spiritually by disrupting the fabric of your household and costing you the joy that you desperately desire and try to achieve by your own hand.

Pride will overthrow compromise if we let it. Pride is a great "distance developer." Pride will have us believing that our way is always right, that it's our way or the highway, and that if we give in, we will be viewed as weak.

Our ministries and our lives are not separate but joined together. It is not a matter of who gets to say what but of what the Lord says. Our positions exist so that they can coexist and be fruitful and multiply the great things of the Lord.

Our ministries are in agreement with each other, and one is not more important than the other. Each is just as important. We are journeying in this thing together, not jockeying for the most likes, accolades, or applause.

Being in one accord is essential to the kingdom of God. Does that mean that you will agree on everything? No, it doesn't. What that does mean is that prayer and answers from the Holy Spirit must be paramount, up-front, and forward in your decision making. When making a determination as to whether you are jockeying or journeying, you must first examine your position, not your marital or job position. The position of your heart must be examined. Are you coming from a position of self-promotion, or are you taking the form of a bond servant (Phil. 2:7–8) and coming in the likeness of Him who humbled himself and became obedient to the point of death?

When we jockey, overtalk, or rudely interject, we are telling our husbands, and those around us, that this is how we are to treat our husbands. We have to remember that God loved them first, and God surely loves them best. They are not our competition, but we are to walk with them in cooperation and collaboration.

SELF-REFLECTION QUESTIONS

What has been the greatest conflict in your marriage thus far? How did you handle or resolve it?

_____

_____

_____

_____

_____

_____

What are some activities you do as individuals that may cause problems within your marriage?

Are there more individual activities than mutual?

_____

_____

_____

_____

_____

_____

What external issues (e.g., job, money, friends) are competing with your marriage internally?

_____

_____

_____

_____

_____

Have you attempted to learn or engage in an activity that your spouse enjoys? Have you tried including your spouse in your activity?

_____
_____
_____
_____
_____
_____

Do you and your spouse pray together regularly? How often? If not, why not?

_____
_____
_____
_____
_____
_____

CHAPTER 7

WALKING INTO MY DESTINY ALONGSIDE A COVENANT-KEEPING GOD

The journeys of marriage and of life in general can be full of adversity. A person's ability to effectively resolve and overcome problems with the help of the Lord undoubtedly transforms his or her inner self for the better. My chapter explains how I have traded ashes for beauty while walking into my destiny alongside a covenant-keeping God.

THEME: TRUST AND HOPE

I CHOSE TO become spiritually prepared before entering a marriage, and it has been one of the best decisions I've ever made. I spent two years after college working on my inner self. I practiced a life of celibacy and spent time enriching an intimate relationship with God. I grew in confidence and felt ready for God to take me to the next phase in my life: marriage. I encourage every woman to make an effort to develop an intimate relationship with God and to feel comfortable asking our Father for help, strength, and rest. You will need it.

Let us face the truth. Most married couples find themselves in situations that are beyond their control. The reason my marriage has not ended in divorce can be attributed to the development and evolvement of my spiritual readiness, which is the skill of calling upon the Lord and relying only on His strength, not my own. We must be dependent on God, our Creator and Maker of Heaven and Earth. Leaning on Him has ultimately made me become a better problem solver and a happier and more fearless individual. Let me give an example of how God solves my problems for me. One morning, my husband brought up the idea of moving the family to Arizona in order to attain a higher-paying job. I was 100 percent against the idea. I gave all the excuses in the book as to why we shouldn't move, such as "Our house is underwater, and we won't be able to sell"; "Our family support system is here"; and "All my doctors are here." But despite all my efforts, my husband was still adamant about moving, even to the point of suggesting he move to Arizona alone. I became anxious and worried. This topic even became a full-blown argument on a number of occasions.

When the worry and anxiety began to get the best of me, I decided to change my strategy. So I started to pray wholeheartedly to God about the issue. A week later, my husband came to me and shared that a colleague of his was facing the same problem that we were having. His colleague was able to compromise with his wife, and they ended up staying in state. I attribute my husband's encounter with his colleague to an act of God because he was more open to staying in state after the encounter. Not only did my husband change his about moving to Arizona, but he even received an irresistible in-state job offer a couple of months later. I thought, What an abundant God I serve. I shouldn't have wasted energy arguing with my husband or spent time worrying over this matter when prayer was the solution. This is just one of many examples of how leaning on God creates solutions to situations that seem impossible for me to solve.

My married life has been through ups and downs. Worry, anxiety, frustration, and fear have been a plague throughout my journey. I am constantly trying to take hold of my identity, dignity, and self-worth. So many different factors in marriage can cause one to stray away from being whom God wants us to be. For instance, some of us enter into marriage envisioning what we want our spouses to be like. "Suzy Homemaker" was what my husband imaged as the ideal wife. Well, I am no Suzy Homemaker, and he knew that going into the marriage. Then why did he marry me? My husband thought I would be a better woman if I were more domestic, but I most certainly did not get my doctorate to have a Suzy life. After digging deeper into my husband's history, I realized Suzy Homemaker was the only image he had of married women when he was growing up. His father was the financial provider, and his mother took care of all the domestic functions in the home. My husband grew up in a very traditional household. But why did my husband hang on to this old paradigm of marriage in this day and age? Why didn't he realize our marriage was different and that I was the one bringing home the bacon? Especially since we had small children, it was totally unrealistic to expect me to carry most of the financial weight of the family as well as be 100 percent domestic. In order for the family to function smoothly, I needed help and support from him. Unfortunately, it was difficult to convince my husband that our current marriage situation needed him to give me domestic support, especially because he had never witnessed his father, or any other man in his culture, performing those types of household duties.

My view on marriage is quite different from his. My mother raised me as a single parent, so I watched her take on both the domestic and provider role. As a result, I grew up with the view that when people marry and have a family, they commit to sharing responsibilities rather than assigning duties according to gender. For years, I took on both the provider and domestic role in my home. Initially, I didn't mind because I had seen my mother do it all, and I had the notion that my husband would love me more if I were more domestic. Interestingly, a compensating situation arose, whereby my husband never gave me a helping hand with the children or in the home and my mother always did. So for a long time, I didn't even realize the dysfunction in my life. As the family grew larger, I couldn't sustain both roles even with my mother's help. The whole marriage became a heavy burden to me. I had worked myself into physical and mental exhaustion. I don't blame my husband or my mother, though. Because my mother was a single mother, she had played both roles and, thus, judged my marriage situation to be normal. As for my husband, he deemed a normal marriage structure to be a domestic woman and a nondomestic man despite not even playing the provider role. Through all this, I finally came to realize through God's help that God wanted me to be a woman different from both my mother and the Suzy Homemaker my husband wanted me to be. This revelation set me free and set me on a path of walking into my destiny alongside a covenant-keeping God.

A covenant is simply a promise or guarantee. Deuteronomy says that "God is a faithful God, keeping his covenant of love to a thousand generation who love him and keep his commandments" (Deut. 7:9). In other words, God is a covenant-keeping God to the faithful. I hold tight to the two covenants in the Bible: the covenant of marriage and the covenant of the blood. The blood covenant is a promise that God has made to choose a people for Himself to bless. This is a promise of eternal blessing through the saving blood of His son, Jesus Christ, and is the basis of my Christian faith. The covenant of marriage is the vows my husband and I took at the altar under God.

In the winter of 2005, my husband and I separated. I had to call upon the Lord to provide me with the spiritual readiness to overcome the separation.

Let me give you some background on the beginning of my marriage. I was newly engaged, and I had it all. I was young, and I had the career. I'd completed my doctorate; landed a six-figure-paying job; got married to a tall, dark, and handsome husband; and had a beautiful baby boy, all within one year! God had done it for me. Things moved very fast, and everything I ever wanted was coming true.

But I stopped worshiping God despite all His blessings shining in my life. I call this period a "derailment," a temporary disruption to my relationship with God. This derailment caused me to have a weakened spirit and clouded judgment. It was like being lost in the dark wilderness of life without God's light to guide me. This period in my life ultimately left me susceptible to the devil and his tactics. I still attended church, but I lacked the heartfelt desire and zeal for God to be in my life. Unfortunately, God became more and more distant in my life. Furthermore, I did not have a prayer strategy, nor did I seek knowledge from the Bible. My marriage went haywire during this time. I was fighting for the right things, but I did not have God's armor on the battlefield. Therefore, I continued to lose the battle in spite of my righteous cause. I became frustrated with my marriage and feared that it wouldn't survive, to say the least. As Ephesians states,

> Finally, be strong in the Lord and in his mighty power. Put on the full armor of God, so that you can take your stand against the devil's schemes. For our struggle is not against flesh and blood, but against the rulers, against the authorities, against the powers of this dark world and against the spiritual forces of evil in the heavenly realms. Therefore put on the full armor of God, so that when the day of evil comes, you may be able to stand your ground, and after you have done everything, to stand. Stand firm then, with the belt of truth buckled around your waist, with the breastplate of righteousness in place, and with your feet fitted with the readiness that comes from the gospel of peace. In addition to all this, take up the shield of faith, with which you

can extinguish all the flaming arrows of the evil one. Take the helmet of salvation and the sword of the Spirit, which is the word of God. (Eph. 6:10–7)

Not only was my personal relationship with God derailed, but my marriage also was built on a weak foundation to begin with. This type of combination leads to divorce. The bottom line is that my husband and I were not strong enough Christians to make God the priority in our union. Isn't it ironic that God, the Creator of the institution of marriage, was put on my back burner? Looking back, I wish I had stood firmly with God and His principles. Prior to getting married, I had spent individual time developing a relationship with God. However, this was not enough. I wish I had attempted to make a three-in-one marriage with Jesus Christ at the center. This would have made it easier to deal with marriage in general.

So how I was able to overcome my derailment, a weak marriage in which we had separated? It was my faith. Faith and strength go hand in hand, especially during times of crisis. During my separation from my husband, I had to draw an incredible amount of strength from the Lord. My separation seemed horrible from the outside looking in. However, I had hope and faith that the Lord could carry me through. I saw myself worshiping and praising God through my storm, and this gave me the confidence I needed to know that God could solve any problem, even my broken marriage, a situation that seemed impossible to solve at the time. As it says in Hebrews, "But without faith it is impossible to please Him, for he who comes to God must believe that He is, and that He is a rewarder of those who diligently seek Him" (Heb. 11:6).

My faith also compelled me to seek God. We can seek God through his Word. The book of Daniel and the ten-day Daniel Fast has been awesome resources for gaining strength and seeing quick results from God. Daniel was thrown into a pit of lions, but an angel kept the lions from eating him because of his faith. The book of Daniel demonstrates how a steadfast faith in God can create immediate solutions in the middle of a storm. I would like to share how I dissect the book of Daniel so that you will not only read it but also meditate on the Word, thus making it more penetrating and real to your personal situation. For the first time, I read the book of Daniel just for understanding. The second time that I read the book, I searched for deeper meaning by taking on characters' roles to understand their feelings. The third and final time I read the book, I assigned the different characters in the book to people from my personal life. Of course, I am always the victorious Daniel. The lion can be a person or any fear you may have. I absolutely cherish the book of Daniel! The combination of the Word, prayer, and fasting is a great tool that can help you solve problems and yield you long-lasting results from God.

Remember that God makes all things beautiful in His time through seasons. So don't give up on marriage so easily. Spiritual readiness is required so that your marriage can be equipped to overcome obstacles or receive all of God's blessings in your due season. There are a number of ways to build your spiritual readiness. Along with consistent prayer, you can seek counsel from positive spiritual leaders in your community. Merely associating with God-fearing married couples can give you new ideas on how to spiritually cope through marriage. God sends people into your life for many reasons. God sent significant people into my life for the sole purpose of helping me bear the cross of marriage. These people are what I call "spiritual vessels," or my support system. I developed a relationship with my coworker during the initial stage of my marriage. She and I worked the graveyard shift together. This Christian woman at work became my first spiritual mentor. She was older and a lot wiser than me. She had also been in the marriage game a lot longer that I had. She could, therefore, understand the trials and tribulations of matrimony, especially because she was going through some of her own.

I loved the relationship because it was mutual and genuine. I trusted her and could talk to her openly about household issues. It felt good to have a consistent person to turn to for honest and godly advice. She taught me that general everyday prayer is a significant component to spiritual readiness. She was the first person to tell me to pray for my marriage, my husband, and myself. This seems like a no-brainer, but it was something that I never done before. What made her so special is that she told me to pray, and she prayed with me every day for an entire six months. As Matthew says, "For where two or three are gathered together in my name, there am I in the midst of them" (Matt. 18:20). I looked forward to our nightly talks and her words of wisdom. One of the most important statements she said was, "The truth is in the Bible. Put all your trust in the Lord and not man and not your husband." These are words I live by, especially when the chips are down and my life experiences are beyond my control. I began to learn not to complain or even have expectations from my husband, but to expect everything from God through His promises and covenants. Oh boy, what a relief it was to know and have confidence in God, the source of every blessing and solution to every problem. This furthered my dependence on the Lord. I encourage you to recognize your marriage-support systems. Thank God for them.

God revealed another important spiritual vessel to me during my separation. God made her known to me in my yoga class, a very unlikely place to meet a person who would help me overcome my battles in my marriage. This woman is special to me because she enlightened me about praying with my whole heart, which entailed bringing out feelings and emotions during prayer. I call her prayer style "warfare prayers." Warfare prayers always yield quality results. This is done by praying in a special way: holding God to His specific covenants and promises while expressing your own personal and current sufferings in the form of the anger, sadness, or bitterness that has occurred as a result of covenants and promises not manifesting in your life. I can attribute my marriage reconciliation to my personal enforcement of the covenants of marriage and the blood. By combining fasting, Bible reading, and warfare prayers, I was able to make God hear my problems loud and clear so that He could solve them.

In November 2013 I was diagnosed with a chronic condition. I honestly thought I would die. It took doctors nearly one week to figure out what was wrong with me. I would hear conflicting reports. One day, they would say I might have cancer; the next day, they would tell me that I probably had an infectious disease or an immune disorder. As I lay in the hospital bed, I thought that whatever I was suffering from could take me out for good. One afternoon my family visited me. I looked into the eyes of my husband, and I saw fear. I looked into the eyes of my children, and I saw the sweet innocence in them, especially as they jumped and played with me on top of the hospital bed. My daughter asked me, "When are you coming home, Mommy?" Silence hit the room because no one knew the answer to that question.

As usual, that night I woke up with night sweats that drenched my pillow, but instead of going back to sleep, I thought about my family, the reflections in their eyes, and all the work that I had to do for them. I began to beg God and pleaded for Him to heal me and save my life. I closed my eyes and wept for God to make me well again. I said, "It's your work I still have yet to do; it's your work I haven't finished on Earth." That night, I had an encounter with the Holy Spirit; "The Lord has heard my plea; the Lord accepts my prayer" (Ps. 6:9). The next morning, a team of doctors came to my room and said, "We know what you have, and it's not cancer, and it's not Ebola." It was a chronic condition that had a known treatment. I was given medication, and within thirty minutes, my body felt stronger. This near-death experience was the beginning of my faith that God can do anything. This experience was also the end of the derailment period in my life because it led to my daily invitation for God's Holy Spirit to come into my life. I pray, and this has been paramount in my acceptance and awareness of my purpose. This one significant encounter with the Holy Spirit touched and transformed me. God's healing was a miracle to me and felt, in my heart, very similar to God parting the Red Sea. I remind myself of this miracle daily so that my heart is fully aware God's capabilities.

A daily invitation of the Holy Spirit to come into your heart leads to living a purpose-driven life and ultimately gives you a sense of fulfillment and satisfaction not only in your marriage but also in your career and daily interactions with people. An invitation to the Holy Spirit to come into my life is not always a walk in the park. Remember that the Holy Spirit led Jesus Christ, our model, in and out of danger. Most importantly, remember that Christ was victorious in every instance of danger. That is why He is a capable deliverer when called upon, for "Do you not know that your body is a temple of the Holy Spirit within you, whom you have from God, and that you are not you own? For you have been purchased at a price. Therefore glorify God in your body" (1 Cor. 6:19–20). I encourage you to invite the Holy Spirit daily into your life, marriage, and home. Be in tune to the change in your life that will result from this action.

Through my forty-five years on Earth, I have finally come to realize that I am truly God's handiwork. I now understand that He holds my destiny in the palm of His hand, and I live for His glory. My destiny involves two things: becoming the woman God wants me to be and positively impacting the lives of my fellow human beings. The journey of marriage is not easy, nor is it meant to be easy. I pray that my openness about my life will help you overcome obstacles faced in your marriage.

Self-Reflection Questions

Do you know any strength-building Bible stories? I encourage you to seek out such stories, like the book of Daniel, that you can reference in your time of need.

_____

_____

_____

_____

_____

_____

Are you the person whom God wants you to be? If not, identify hindering factors in your life that are preventing you from being that person you are called to be.

_____

_____

_____

_____

_____

_____

Can you identify your spiritual support system? Who are the Simons in your life who can help you bear your cross?

_____

_____

_____

_____

_____